$\mathcal{T}$he Hockey Hall of Fame

has embarked on a new phase of its historic journey, one which has led

us to a state-of-the-art complex in downtown Toronto, Canada.

As hockey's official historian, we are proud to celebrate the coming

of age of our new facility with this magnificent book,

Hockey Hall of Fame Legends.

Selected members from the Hall's honour roll provide the inspiration

for this vibrant visual history. The beauty of their artifacts

and the stories they tell unfolds before us in a unique testament

to the legends of the great game.

We trust you will enjoy, as we have, this powerful legacy to

the members of the Hockey Hall of Fame.

Scotty Morrison
Chairman, Hockey Hall of Fame

Hockey Hall of Fame Founding Sponsors:

Bell Canada	Ford Motor Company of Canada	Household Financial	TSN, The Sports Network
Coca-Cola Ltd.	Imperial Oil	Molson Breweries	Toronto Sun Publishing Corporation

Hockey Hall of Fame Legends

— THE OFFICIAL BOOK —

Author, Michael McKinley

Photographer, Derik Murray

Designer, Ken Koo

•

Foreword, Ken Dryden

VIKING

Viking Press/Opus Productions Inc.

VIKING Published by the Penguin Group and Opus Productions Inc.

Penguin Books Canada Ltd, 10 Alcorn Avenue, Toronto, Ontario, Canada M4V 3B2
Penguin Books Ltd, 27 Wrights Lane, London W8 5TZ, England
Viking Penguin, a division of Penguin Books USA Inc., 375 Hudson Street, New York, New York 10014, U.S.A.
Penguin Books Australia Ltd, Ringwood, Victoria, Australia
Penguin Books (NZ) Ltd, 182-190 Wairau Road, Auckland 10, New Zealand

Penguin Books Ltd, Registered Offices: Harmondsworth, Middlesex, England

Opus Productions Inc., 300 West Hastings Street, Vancouver, British Columbia, Canada V6B 1K6

First Published 1993

10 9 8 7 6 5 4 3 2 1

Printed and bound in Hong Kong by Book Art Inc., Toronto

Canadian Cataloguing In Publication Data
McKinley, Michael, 1961–
Hockey Hall of Fame Legends

Includes bibliographical references and index.
ISBN O-670-85258-9

1. Hockey players - Biography - Pictorial works.
2. Hockey - History - Pictorial works.
I. Murray, Derik A., 1956– . II. Title.

GV846.5M25 1993   796.962′092′2   C93-093907-7

A Viking/Opus Productions Book

Contents

Foreword

Halls of Fame are about history, and history is stories. About people, about the things people use. I love to look at old objects. Touch them if I can, and hold onto them long enough to start thinking and wondering, to create my own stories:

The hockey stick of 1899, one-piece, thick, straight, short-shafted like a field hockey stick, made to push, sling forward, hit, above all not to break. Too short and unyielding for slapshots. A practical instrument before arenas and money, before forward passing was permitted. The sticks of Rocket Richard and Gordie Howe more than 50 years later, thinner, longer-shafted, yet not much different. Cracks in the blade, tape ripped, more black collision marks than a single game can produce, still a practical compromise. The modern stick, thin, tapered, curved, nearly unmarked, with a slender bendable shaft. Able to turn the force of the body into something far greater. Built for power, shooting, subtlety, and an uncompromising game that rewards both. A puck launcher.

The early skate blade, not much changed from Hans Brinker's on the Dutch canals, sturdy metal attached to a wooden base connected to a separate boot. Decades later, Frank Foyston's skate, permanently attached to a leather boot, still long, thick, flat and unrockered like a goalie skate. A solid, durable base for balance, on rutted pre-Zambonied ice; with so much blade anchored to the ice, no quick turns or changes in direction, made for straight headlong rushes and for lumbering, body-checking defencemen able to move in the same straight lines to stop them.

And if big-bladed players can't dance, the puck must dance, so the stickhandler is king. And so is speed, durability, guts, and a relentless "pick yourself up and try again" spirit. King Clancy on the Toronto Maple Leaf program: His grin of combat, his signature posture, one hand on his stick, the puck pushed ahead, heading straight to the net or a defenceman's hip, either is fine with him.

One of the game's greatest goaltenders, Hall of Famer Ken Dryden, donned the bleu, blanc et rouge of the Montreal Canadiens from 1970 to 1979. Dryden was inducted into the Hall of Fame in 1983.

Facing Page: All time great Frank Foyston's skates and gloves, circa 1928, and Seattle Metropolitans jersey, circa 1917.

Joe Hall's contract, from 10 November, 1918 to 25 March, 1919, from winter freeze to spring thaw, before technology changed the seasons. The hockey card. A visual image before television. Something to look at while listening to that big round-topped box and the voice of Foster Hewitt.

The prehistoric goalie, his thin, wicketkeeper's leg pads, stick and not much else. How does he cope with pain and danger? Is he a different breed? From more physical times, does he have different expectations of pain, is the worst of it deadened by the cold of unheated rinks? Or maybe his risk was less. The puck couldn't be shot so hard with club-like sticks. In a controlled, straight-ahead game, shots come from further. There is less confusion at the net, fewer deflections, screen shots, rebounds; there is less danger.

Or maybe his "stand-up" style, the way every goalie is taught to play. Maybe it is really more for safety than effectiveness. A way to put an unprotected face as far from the puck as possible. Later a catching glove to

catch, *and* protect; leg and torso pads, thicker to meet the demands of better sticks and shooter's skills, but billowing wider, leaving body form behind, *to protect the net.*

And Jacques Plante's mask, fiberglass against bare skin; the cage mask, resting safely away from the skin. How do they change things? What happens when finally a goalie becomes fully protected, when pain and danger are eliminated? When the mask becomes just another blocking instrument like leg pads and gloves, when a goalie can play the way the action determines? The need for the "stand-up" style disappears; the forever compromise of safety and effectiveness ends.

Just old, lifeless things that determine the game as much as its players.

How things were and why, and why they are today.

And what about the wool sweater, and Gordie Howe's patched leather gloves? I have some thoughts, but I'll leave you to your own. In each of the remarkable pictures of this book are stories just waiting for you to write.

Enjoy yourself.

Ken Dryden, March 15, 1993, Toronto.

HOCKEY

Introduction

It is a game of speed, of grace, of passion and truly a game of legends. From its humble beginnings well over a century ago, hockey has risen to become a game of near mythic status, personified by its heroes and legends—the players and plays of a lifetime.

The Hockey Hall of Fame enshrines the game's greatest players and celebrates their true excellence. Only the very best are represented in the Hockey Hall of Fame, an honour roll that boasts the greatest names in hockey: "Cyclone" Taylor, Howie Morenz, "Rocket" Richard, "King" Clancy, Gordie Howe, Bobby Orr, Bobby Hull and Ken Dryden, to name but a few.

Featuring exclusively created photographs of the Hockey Hall of Fame's unparalleled collection of artifacts and memorabilia, *Hockey Hall of Fame Legends* presents a dynamic visual history of the game and its illustrious heroes.

In concert with these elegant, sophisticated photographs, *Hockey Hall of Fame Legends* evokes the drama, passion and triumph of hockey, combining solid historical research with the spirit of myth and legend. This book does not seek to offer an encyclopedic account of ice hockey but rather to capture the essence of its personality over the past century, as drawn from the formidable archives of the Hockey Hall of Fame. With this lavish book, you can follow the game from its romantic origins on the frozen lakes and ponds of Canada to its robust, barnstorming years at the turn of the century and onward to the Jazz Age, World War II, the golden era of the "Original Six" and the heady days of expansion.

Readers will see Lord Stanley's glittering trophy of 1893, the oldest trophy competed for by professional athletes in North America. Here is the frayed, game-worn jersey of Hap Holmes, goaltender for the 1917 Seattle Metropolitans, the first American team to win the Stanley Cup, and the skates worn by George Vezina, the tragic "Chicoutimi Cucumber" whose greatness is immortalized in the Vezina Trophy, the highest award for NHL goaltending excellence.

Hockey Hall of Fame Legends provides an arena in which the laws of time, narrative and possibility become one with the game. The stories and photographs that grace these pages can be revisited as often as we wish, each time providing a view of the game and its heroes, as unique and varied as our imaginations.

The Beginning

Senior Championship
Trophy, circa 1886.
Left: Artifacts of a bygone
era; skates, stick and
puck from the mid 1800s.

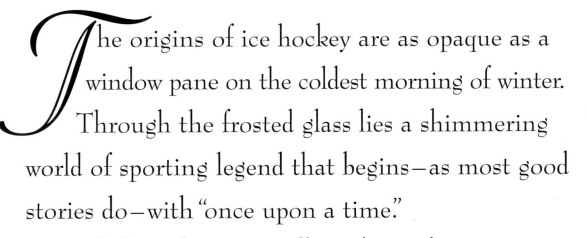he origins of ice hockey are as opaque as a
window pane on the coldest morning of winter.
Through the frosted glass lies a shimmering
world of sporting legend that begins—as most good
stories do—with "once upon a time."

People have been propelling themselves across ice ever since
they first encountered winter's frozen ponds and lakes. The need
to travel from here to there spawned possibilities for pleasure
and sport, as people came to see the ice as something more than
a temporary winter road.

William Fitzstephen's *Description of the Most Notable Citie of London* has Londoners revelling on ice at the end of the 12th century: "When the great fenne or moore which watereth the citie of London on the north Side is frozen many young men play on the yce...some tye bones to their feet [and] do slide swiftlie as a bird flyeth in the aire or an arrow out of a crossbow." Breughel (the Younger) depicts people skating on bones in a 1512 painting, and by the early 17th century, the Dutch had invented the metal skate. Supporters of England's Charles I, who had fled to Holland during Oliver Cromwell's Protectorate, brought the ice skate home when the monarchy was restored in 1660.

As the great powers of Europe pursued Empire, their social trappings came with them. English troops introduced the metal skate to Canada in the late 17th century, and by the middle of the 19th century, ice skating had become a popular North American pastime. Toronto built its first covered rink in 1858, and the world's first artificial ice arena, known as The Glacarium, was built in London, England, in 1876. The tiny 24-by-40-foot rink, which became the private reserve of England's aristocracy, showcased form rather than action. Its patrons, it seems, could do little more than glide a few feet while watching and being watched by their peers.

There is no anointed date that the historian can point to as ice hockey's origin, but by the early 19th century the game as North Americans know it was in its embryonic state. A 1930s British source quixotically claims ice hockey originated at Windsor Castle in the freezing winter of 1853. Apparently, Royal Family members and Household Guard officers slid across the royal ice, using crude sticks to shoot a wooden plug. Prince Albert played goal, while Queen Victoria, amused no doubt, looked on from the side.

Though romantic and fabulous, the claim speaks more about the nature of colonialism than it does about hockey. If the Royals and their soldiers did play a crude form of ice hockey at Windsor Castle in 1853, it was because British troops, garrisoned in the Dominion of "Canada," had brought it back to England with them.

McGill University's first hockey team prepares to scrimmage with hurley-style sticks at Montreal's Crystal Palace Skating Rink, 1881.

The game was so popular in Nova Scotia by 1853 that it incurred the wrath of a Halifax religious community who called it "Sabbath Desecration." Local children were harassed by a man they called "The Dragon," who was paid to chase them from a popular local pond on Sundays.

Ice hockey evolved from any number of games played with sticks and a ball, games that transcend any particular culture. A marble relief in the Athenian acropolis, fifth century B.C., which Aristotle himself must have passed while paying homage to the gods, shows two men holding sticks with a ball between them as if preparing for a face-off. Ireland, Scotland, England, Russia and Scandinavia have all produced ball-and-stick games that, when played on ice, can be considered the forerunners of hockey. Indigenous peoples of eastern Canada played a game called baggataway, better known as lacrosse, and the word "hockey" is thought to derive from the Iroquois word "hoghee." The Micmac tribe played a game on ice variously using an animal's knucklebone, a piece of wood or a "horse apple" as a puck, while the stick was a whittled tree branch. The Micmacs became famous as hockey-stick makers and supplied superb sticks to the developing North American game right up until the end of the 19th century.

The game played in Canada early in the 1800s was known in English as "hurley," "bandy," or "shinty"– all names of European ball-and-stick games. The game on ice was more a hybrid of field hockey and lacrosse,

involving two teams of 11 to 15 players, most of whom would be wearing skates. The game began when the player acting as referee threw the ball into the middle of the ice. Using short, curved sticks not more than two inches wide, players would try to hit the ball through a goal marked by two rocks about the size of curling stones. These were placed four to six feet apart and defended by a goalkeeper.

As hockey in Canada grew in popularity, several cities vied for the honour of being the birthplace of the game that has become so much a part of the Canadian soul. Dalhousie University historian A. J. Young marshals a formidable case for Nova Scotia, citing the schoolboy experiences of Thomas Chandler Haliburton, author of *Sam Slick* and an 1810

Queen's University hockey champions of 1888 upheld the resolute spirit of amateurism that coloured the early years of hockey.

graduate of King's Collegiate in Windsor, Nova Scotia. Haliburton, recalling his school days many years later in an English journal, writes, "The boys let out racin', yellin', hollerin' and whoopin' like mad with pleasure, and the playground, and the game at bass in the fields, or hurley on the long pond on the ice."

Yet the flourishing game of hockey was by no means exclusive to Nova Scotia. On the last Saturday of February 1837, the year rebellion shook both Upper and Lower Canada, a pitched battle on ice took place between Montreal's Dorchester and Uptown clubs. John Knox, the 84-year-old son of Michael Knox, who had played in the 1837 match for Uptown, related the story to the *Montreal Star* in 1941 from records passed down by his father. Dorchester scored first, after which their jubilant fans flooded onto the ice and refused to leave. Dorchester was awarded the championship, a fact that grated on Montreal's budding hockey community.

On the second Saturday in March, on a rink below Montreal's Bleury and Dorchester streets, the "champions" defended their title against a team of mainly French-Canadian players calling themselves Les Canadiens. Each club iced eight players: goal, point, cover-point, centre, rover, home, right side and left side. Aside from the rich historical significance of a francophone team called Les Canadiens playing an anglophone team in a volatile and bloody year, the fact that both clubs had names, structure and a coterie of fans suggests that organized hockey came of age in Montreal early in the 19th century.

Kingston, Ontario, also contends that it holds the roots of the modern game of ice hockey. Captain James

3158—HOCKEY MATCH, VICTORIA RINK, MONTREAL.

The Montreal Victorias played a home game in 1893 against their rivals, the Montreal AAA's, who would become the first winners of the Stanley Cup in that same year.

The 1895 Stanley-Cup-winning Montreal Victorias pose proudly with Lord Stanley's championship "Jug" and its predecessor, the Senior Championship Trophy.

Sutherland, an early hockey organizer and honoured member of the Hockey Hall of Fame, claimed that the Royal Canadian Rifles played the first game of hockey on Kingston harbour in the winter of 1855. A 1942 Canadian government report on hockey's origin and development in Canada supports the claim, though that document states the game was played by two sides of 50 players each dragooned from the Royal Canadian Rifles stationed at British garrisons in Kingston and Halifax. Even so, the high number of players suggests a rather informal game of shinny, rather than the organized match between the two Montreal clubs in 1837.

The first advertisement for a public ice hockey match is found in the *Montreal Gazette* in 1875, announcing a game at the Victoria Skating Rink that evening, March 3, between "two nines" from among the member clubs of the Montreal hockey fraternity. The pitch cleverly sought both to reassure the timid and provoke the brave by promising an exciting and just ever-so-slightly dangerous spectacle: "Good fun may be expected, as some of the players are reputed to be exceedingly expert at the game. Some fears have been expressed on the part of the intended spectators that accidents will be likely to occur through the ball flying about in a too lively manner…but we understand that the game will be played with a flat, circular piece of wood, thus preventing all danger of its leaving the surface of the ice."

By 1880, there were three organized teams in Montreal, along with dozens of recreational clubs, and the institutional game was gaining popularity in Quebec City and Ottawa. The Montreal Winter Carnival of 1883 held the world's first ice hockey tournament to showcase the "new" game. Montreal's Victoria Rink and

One of Canada's first organized hockey clubs, the Montreal Victorias, had by 1896 become the dominant force in the game, that year winning the Senior Championship Trophy and the Stanley Cup.

McGill University competed with a team from Quebec City for the Bedouin Cup, and the fact that a trophy now existed to recognize a champion further enshrined hockey as a fixture in the Canadian sporting world.

Yet the first ice hockey tournament was not without its problems, plagued as it was by poor weather, poor ice and time and space conflicts between hockey games and other carnival events. Players competing in that first tournament had to dodge an ice grotto, a bandstand and a snow sculpture, all located at centre ice at one time or another.

The following year, a team from Ottawa replaced the team from Quebec City and nearly won the Bedouin Cup. Known as the Rideau Hall Rebels, they were led by James Creighton, a McGill-educated Halifax native credited with developing the game in the Ottawa region. Two members of the Rebels were sons of Canada's Governor General, Lord Stanley of Preston, who would soon become part of hockey legend himself.

The game became increasingly popular and sophisticated. By the Montreal Winter Carnival of 1886, a meeting was called between representatives of teams from Montreal, Quebec City, Ottawa, Toronto and Kingston to codify the game's rules and further establish its legitimacy and permanence. The 14-point

Montreal Rules established ice hockey as an "onside" game, which meant only lateral and backward passes were allowed. Each team iced seven men: one goalie—without benefit of pads; two defencemen, known as "point" and "cover-point"; a rover, who switched from offence to defence as play dictated; and three forwards. The rover disappeared from the eastern Canadian game circa World War I, but lingered in the Pacific Coast Hockey Association until 1922. Late 19th century games consisted of two half-hour periods with a 10-minute rest period in between, and play featured a dump-and-chase structure: the point and cover-point would shoot the puck from their own end high into the air to centre ice, then their forwards would move the puck laterally toward the opponent's goal. Blue lines and the red line did not yet exist, so the puck carrier determined the floating offside "line."

With the defenders out of the play, the puck carrier was much like the ball carrier in rugby and would be swarmed by members of the opposing team who would knock him off the puck and chase it back down the ice. The players' long-bladed skates did not have rockers, which limited their movement, and as no ice resurfacing machines existed, the buildup of snow throughout the match slowed down both players and puck.

Paramount to all was the amateur status of the players, as true sportsmen competed in the spirit of ancient Greece, out of love for the sport and the reward of a game well and fairly played.

By 1890, two organized amateur leagues existed, the Amateur Hockey Association of Canada and the Ontario Hockey Association (formed respectively in 1886 and 1890). Teams competed for the Senior Championship Trophy, the premier hockey trophy in Canada. But that was about to change as the game became wildly popular at all levels of class and consciousness in Canada, eventually catching the eye of Lord Stanley, who would endow the game with one of the most coveted trophies in sport—and for a sport that would soon become "professional."

Young boy striking the classic hockey pose, circa 1893.

The Stanley Cup

1902 Stanley Cup program featuring the Toronto Wellingtons and the Winnipeg Victorias. **Left:** Lord Stanley of Preston and the original Stanley Cup bowl.

On March 18, 1892, at a festive dinner for the Ottawa Amateur Athletic Association, Lord Kilcoursie, aide to Canada's Governor General Lord Stanley of Preston and a member of the Rideau Hall Rebels ice hockey team, rose from the table and clinked his spoon on his brandy snifter. After subduing the garrulous sportsmen, he read a message from the governor general that would establish one of the sporting world's great icons: "I have for some time been thinking that it would be a good thing if there were a challenge cup which should be held from

Frank McGee

One-eyed Frank McGee, who played his brief but prolific four seasons with the Ottawa Senators after losing his eye to the butt end of a stick, still holds the record for scoring the most goals in a Stanley Cup game. Ottawa's flashy "Silver Seven," a nickname born in 1903 when their manager gave each player a silver nugget, faced robust Yukon prospectors after silver of a different sort in 1905 when they defended their Stanley Cup title against an upstart crew from Dawson City. The northerners had dogsledded 400 miles to Whitehorse, shipped down to Seattle, then caught the cross-continental train to Ottawa on a 23-day odyssey that had them playing the night after they arrived, only to receive a 23–2 pasting at the hands of McGee and the Silver Seven. McGee scored an unequalled 14 goals, eight of which came consecutively in eight minutes and 20 seconds, and ensured the Silver Seven's third straight Stanley Cup. McGee hid his optical deficiency well enough to earn him the rank of lieutenant and a place in the trenches at the Somme, where he was killed in action on September 16, 1916.

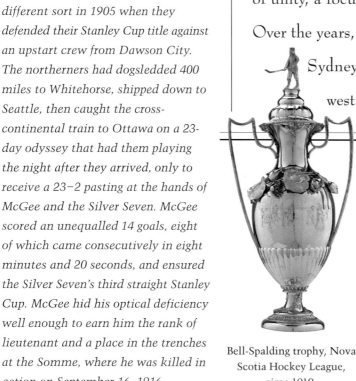

Bell-Spalding trophy, Nova Scotia Hockey League, circa 1910.

First tube skate, made in Canada, circa 1900.

year to year by the champion hockey team in the dominion of Canada."

Lord Stanley's Dominion Challenge Trophy, the oldest award competed for by professional athletes in North America, would come to be known around the world as The Stanley Cup, ice hockey's symbol of excellence.

And it *was* a good thing for a young country and a young sport. By establishing a challenge trophy, Lord Stanley also established a sense of unity, a focus and purpose for athletes in Canada's far-flung regions. Over the years, teams from Dawson City, Yukon, Victoria, B.C., and Sydney, Nova Scotia, all made the trek north, south, east or west in pursuit of the Cup, the distance made small by the greatness of the prize.

Lord Stanley's sons Arthur and Edward are credited with turning their father into an ice hockey fan (as well as with establishing a team in England that would include two future kings, several dukes and a rabble of aristocrats). But Lord Stanley's bequest was more a testament to the flourishing of ice hockey in Canada from 1888 to 1893: the Ontario Hockey Association was formed in 1890; a league in Winnipeg sprung up in 1892; and within the next five years two leagues in Nova Scotia as well as one in New York City were born.

The original Stanley Cup was a silver bowl lined with gold, which was purchased in England off the shelf of the G. H. Collis Co. on London's posh Regent Street for 10 guineas, or $48.67. Two Ottawa citizens, Sheriff John Sweetland and Phillip David Ross, were put in charge of the new trophy as its trustees.

On February 18, 1893, Ottawa and the Montreal Amateur Athletic Association, who had each lost only one game all season, purportedly faced off for the championship, which Montreal won 7–1. Yet newspaper reports at the time made no mention of Lord Stanley's trophy, and at the end of the season, an Ottawa player said his team intended to challenge the Montreal AAA's to another match to decide the Amateur Hockey Association of Canada championship, for which they "believed" the governor general had given a cup.

The rematch was never played, and in May 1893 the *Montreal Gazette* finally published conditions for the competition and presentation of the Stanley Cup. The paper also announced that the Montreal AAA's would be the first recipients as they had defeated all who had challenged them in the season past. The trophy was duly awarded to the president of the Montreal Amateur Athletic Association, who neglected to inform the Stanley Cup committee that the Montreal AAA's hockey team had quit the organization over which he presided. But neither he nor the association saw a conflict in this and they kept the Cup anyway.

The Cup's trustees did not see the situation in quite the same light. In February 1894, they informed the Montreal AAA's in a flurry of letters that it would be a very good idea if it handed the Cup over to its winners. The rechristened Montreal Hockey Club finally got its prize, and shortly after managed to retain it by defeating the Ottawa Capitals 3–1 in the first true Stanley Cup match. The *Montreal Gazette* reported that 5,000 people attended, the ice was good, and "the referee forgot to see many things."

There were 57 challenges for the Stanley Cup—also known affectionately as the "Jug"—from teams across the country in leagues as

Toronto Blueshirts 1914 championship ribbon.

Decorative medallion worn by Bill McGimsie of the Kenora Thistles, 1907 Stanley Cup champions.

Billy McGimsie

Billy McGimsie wrote in a 1962 letter to then Hockey Hall of Fame curator Bobby Hewitson that his "ambition when I started was to play on a winning Stanley Cup team, and I had three cracks at it." McGimsie learned his hockey at school in the town of Kenora, Ontario (pop. 10,000). As no higher education facilities existed near Kenora at the turn of the century, McGimsie's school days ended early, and so he forked out two dollars to join the Kenora Thistles Hockey Club. With comic irony, McGimsie's former school then challenged the Thistles to a game, and Billy saw a chance to impress his old schoolmates. But as McGimsie had skated for both teams, each side suddenly saw a conflict of interest in letting the talented goal scorer play, so McGimsie warmed the bench. The Thistles lost the game, then the entire school team signed on with the Thistles, thus forming the crew that would bring the Stanley Cup to Kenora in January 1907—on their third crack. Kenora became the smallest town ever to win the Cup and further distinguished itself by featuring four future Hall of Fame members: Art Ross, Si Griffis, Tom Hooper and Billy McGimsie.

Portland Rosebuds souvenir pennant.

Ernie "Moose" Johnson

Montreal native Ernest Moose Johnson led his Portland Rosebuds to the 1916 Pacific Coast Hockey Association championship and then into Montreal to face the Canadiens for the Stanley Cup, making the Rosebuds the first American team to compete for hockey's most coveted trophy. Canada's first sporting Moose won his nickname while playing for Lester Patrick's Victoria Aristocrats–his hulking size and seemingly endless hockey stick gave him a 99-inch reach and a certain superhuman stature.

Johnson had already won four Stanley Cups playing cover-point for the Montreal Wanderers, but he was not to achieve a fifth with the Rosebuds as they lost the series to the Canadiens. Still, Johnson considered the fact that he had a hockey career at all to be a bonus, for, as he later wrote, "I think I was the only hockey player that ever played with his fingers on the right hand missing." The man celebrated for his reach and checking skills had lost his fingers after receiving a 2,300-volt shock of electricity in 1900.

Montreal Victorias Hockey Club pin, early 1900s.

various as the Eastern Canada Amateur Hockey Association, the National Hockey Association and the Pacific Coast Hockey Association between 1893 and 1926, when it became the property of the National Hockey League. As each league had its own rules–sometimes with minor variations and sometimes not–the difference in league rules was emphasized in Stanley Cup play since series games would alternate between the rules governing the league from which the Cup's competitors came. The Winnipeg Victorias of 1896 were the first western Canadian team to bear the Cup aloft in triumph; the Thistles of Kenora (pop. 10,000) were from the smallest town to ever win the Cup; the Montreal Wanderers of 1907 were the first team to inscribe the names of all their players on the Cup; the 1915 Vancouver Millionaires were the first PCHA team to win the Cup; and the Seattle Metropolitans of 1917 were the first team to carry the Cup home to the United States. By 1929, not an inch of space was left on the football-sized bowl to immortalize the names of the victors, and the Cup began to grow tall and thin with the addition of a silver base to allow room for commemoration of future winners. In 1947, it grew fatter, featuring uneven silver bands bearing the names of the victorious, but by the 1960s the septuagenarian trophy was showing its age and in danger of breaking, so the NHL commissioned Carl Peterson, a Montreal silversmith, to produce a duplicate of the original bowl, a reproduction so expertly done that years passed before the switch became widely known.

Considering some of the indignities suffered by the Stanley Cup at the hands of impulsive and sometimes forgetful celebrants, it's surprising that the Cup wasn't replaced several times during its first century.

Lord Stanley's gift was booted into Ottawa's Rideau Canal by a turn-of-the-century player responding to a drunken dare, but, since the canal was frozen at the time, the Cup wasn't badly hurt or lost to the depths. It was once left at a photographer's studio and used as a flowerpot by his wife; it has been stolen by pranksters; it has even been left on a snowbank on the Côte des Neiges by celebrating Montreal Canadiens who stopped to change a tire and drove off leaving hockey's Holy Grail behind.

With bittersweet irony, Lord Stanley never saw the presentation of his legacy to ice hockey and to Canada. Early in 1893 his older brother died and Stanley was obliged to return to England forever, there to assume his new title—the Earl of Derby.

Yet his amateur trophy, which preceded tennis's Davis Cup by seven years and baseball's Temple Cup by one, would quickly become the prize pursued by professional hockey players, as the game wove itself into the economic fabric of North America. A vast hierarchy of both organization and excellence was evolving and the sport was soon ready to enter the marketplace as an entertainment people would pay to see. Hockey talent was now a marketable commodity, for sale to the highest bidder. The game inevitably crossed that sociological line between amateur and professional to become a business, and Lord Stanley's legacy would go along with it.

Canadian Hockey League Championship Trophy, won by the Cobalt Opera House team in 1908.

Hobey Baker

Hobart Amery "Hobey" Baker was hockey's first American superstar. Born in 1892 to a wealthy Pennsylvania family, the gifted skater and stick-handler became known in the U.S. as the King of Hockey, and legend attached itself to him as naturally as he attached himself to the game. The Princeton team he captained was known as "Hobey Baker and the Tigers," and it was said that as soon as the puck was on his stick he never needed to look at it again. Once, after being checked up and over the boards, he ran along the bench, leapt into the play, picked up the loose puck and scored. An old Princetonian's memoirs recalled him "as near being what every male would like to think himself in looks and actions as it is possible for one man to be. Everything about him was out of a storybook. He was the perfect college hero." In this heroic tradition, Baker won the Croix de Guerre for valour under fire while flying his black-and-orange plane—Princeton's colours—with the fabled Escadrille Lafayette in World War I. The award was made posthumously, as Baker crashed and died on December 21, 1918, while taking one last flight before being shipped home.

Souvenir game puck, OHA senior champions, Toronto Wellingtons, 1899–1900.

Hod Stuart

Big, genial William Hodgson "Hod" Stuart was one of hockey's most complete defencemen, able to skate, shoot, play make and play break, and, as Hall of Fame referee Chaucer Elliott put it, "a good fellow as well."

Stuart began his hockey career with his Hall of Fame brother Bruce in Ottawa in 1899. His clean, punishing checks and long reach frustrated opponents; his end-to-end rushes dazzled crowds. Stuart then signed a contract in North America's first rough-and-tumble pro league, starring on Michigan's Portage Lake and Calumet teams, as well as in Pittsburgh, and becoming a crusader for respectable salaries and playing conditions. His superb offensive gifts earned him much unpleasantly tactile attention from opposing teams, and after a particularly bloody and mean-spirited game between Pittsburgh and the Michigan "Soo" in 1906, a disgusted Stuart finally accepted a longstanding offer from the Montreal Wanderers at rinkside.

Montreal welcomed Hod as "the greatest hockey player in the world," but he would win only one Stanley Cup with the Wanderers. For on the hot afternoon of June 23, 1907, Stuart went swimming in the Bay of Quinte with friends, dove into the water, struck his head on a submerged rock, and was killed instantly. What is thought to be hockey's first benefit game was held in his memory the following season.

•

John L. "Doc" Gibson

After graduating from Detroit Medical School, Ontario native J. L. "Doc" Gibson set up a dental practice in Houghton, a small town in Michigan's Copper Country, known as "the Canada of the United States" because of its harsh winters. But Gibson, also an excellent defenceman famed for his clean but bruising body checks, managed to establish—between pulling teeth and filling cavities—the world's first professional hockey league. The International Hockey League of 1903-7 comprised teams from Pittsburgh, Houghton, Calumet and both the Canadian and American "Soo." Gibson's Portage Lake squad of 1905 was one of the most stellar hockey teams ever assembled, variously featuring future Hall of Famers Bruce and Hod Stuart, Riley Hern and Cyclone Taylor. The Portage Lake team challenged Ottawa and Montreal to championship series in 1905 and 1906, but was twice refused.

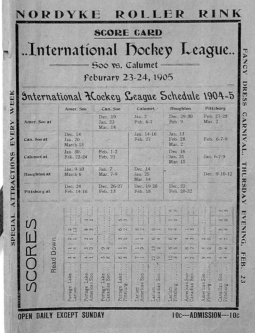

International Hockey League souvenir mini sticks and score card, circa 1905.

The Canadian clubs then enticed the Portage Lake stars back home, and Gibson also returned to Canada, leaving behind his legacy as the "Father of Hockey" in northern Michigan.

•

Game puck from the Ottawa Senators' 5–4 victory over the Montreal Victorias, February 9, 1901

•

Frank Patrick

One of modern hockey's guiding geniuses, Frank Patrick was a superlative combination of athletic prowess, philosophical ingenuity and vision. A stalwart of the McGill University hockey team and a Stanley Cup referee at age 20, he was also a formidable puckhandler and rushing defenceman for the Renfrew Millionaires. This was the man who dreamed of ice hockey on the balmy west coast and so created the Pacific Coast Hockey Association with brother Lester in 1911, building Canada's first artificial ice arena in Vancouver for $350,000. The Denman Street Arena seated 10,000 people, and from here, the largest building in the country, Frank Patrick owned, managed, coached and played defence for the Vancouver Millionaires, marshalling them to their first and only Stanley Cup in 1915.

In the spring of 1912, the eastern champion Quebec Bulldogs came to play an exhibition series in Vancouver. Forward passing did not yet exist, and the coast league's seven-man hockey clashed with Quebec's six-man version, getting the game off to a sluggish start. The referee called 11 quick offsides due to confused passing by the centre to the rover. As the crowd began to jeer, Patrick came up with the idea that a centre ice area should exist in which there could be no offsides, and so the blue line was born.

The astute Patrick would later legalize the forward pass in defensive zones, again to maintain fluidity and excitement; he knew the importance of keeping hockey entertaining and thus profitable. And so his PCHA innovations continued: unlimited substitutions; numbered uniforms; penalties for checking into the boards; the penalty shot; freedom of movement for goalies, who had previously been forbidden to drop to their knees; the blue line; forward passing; and a play-off system eventually copied by many other sports.

Frank Patrick's Imperial Tobacco watercolour trading card, circa 1910–1911.

Mickey Ion

Fred J. "Mickey" Ion was one of hockey's most brashly quick-witted and fearless referees. Ion's professional lacrosse career took him to the west coast, where he refereed his first professional hockey game in New Westminster, B.C., in 1913. Known as the Iron Man of Hockey, Ion would referee four games a week by himself travelling between Portland and Saskatoon. Frank Patrick, co-founder with his brother Lester of the Pacific Coast Hockey Association, was so impressed by Ion's endurance and judiciousness that he moved "The Mick" up through the PCHA and eventually to the NHL. The fair, impartial Ion was rarely in trouble with the fans, though Patrick recalled an occasion in Seattle when a belligerent spectator screamed that Ion was so blind he couldn't see the end of his nose. Ion stopped the play, skated up to the fan and advised him in a few short-syllable words that he would be wise to keep his mouth shut. The astonished and chastened fan turned to his friends and said, "Imagine him picking me out of a crowd of 5,000."

228th Battalion

Hockey legends such as Frank and Lester Patrick may have been turned away from the Canadian army because their contribution to the nation's morale was best made on ice, but by the autumn of 1916 many players had been accepted for active service, and Frank McGee and Allan "Scotty" Davidson had already been killed in action. The 228th Battalion, or Northern Fusiliers, now comprised many Toronto and Northern Ontario hockey stars, so when they applied to the National Hockey Association for membership, their extraordinary request was granted. The 228th skated onto Toronto ice for their first match December 27, 1916, wearing khaki uniforms and the regimental badge, and defeated Ottawa 10–7.

Referee's bell, circa 1920.

In fact, the 228th won their first four games, tallying 40 goals and earning stars George and Howard MacNamara the sobriquet "The Dynamite Twins." By the end of January 1917, the 228th stood in third place with six wins and four losses—one win less and one loss more than the first-place Montreal Canadiens—and had a league-leading "goals-for" total of 70. The 228th never got the chance to complete the schedule; they were shipped to France in February 1917 just in time to participate in some of the bloodiest Canadian campaigns of the war. ●

The Arena Cup was the championship trophy of the Eastern Canada Amateur Hockey Association from 1906 to 1908.

Dan Bain

Donald H. "Dan" Bain, "Canada's Athlete" of the last half of the 19th century, came from a school of amateur athletics that seems as lost to us as the century in which he lived. He triumphed as Manitoba's roller-skating and cycling champion. He was Winnipeg's top gymnast and Canada's trapshooting title holder. And he also won championships in pairs figure skating, lacrosse and ice hockey, captaining the Winnipeg Victorias to two Stanley Cups.

Bain began his hockey career in 1895 with the Victorias, a superlative crew with whom he excelled as a skater, stickhandler and scorer. When the Victorias went east in 1895 to play their counterparts, the Montreal Victorias, they had not yet heard that the Stanley Cup had become emblematic of Canadian amateur hockey supremacy and could be challenged for. The following year the Vics, resplendent in their bright scarlet uniforms, went back to Montreal with their eye firmly on the "Jug." Backstopped by Whitey Merritt in his cricket pads and led by Bain with three goals, Winnipeg beat the Montreal Vics to triumphantly bring the Stanley Cup west for the very first time. Delirious Winnipeg fans, true to the promises of a "hot time" they had made in telegrams to their victorious heroes, fêted the returning champs by drawing them through Winnipeg's streets in carriages.

Bain's Winnipeg team would challenge for the Stanley Cup three more times. In the chivalric amateur spirit of the time, the 1900 Montreal Shamrocks threw a dinner for the team they had defeated by one goal and inscribed on the commemorative dinner card that Winnipeg had played "the finest hockey ever witnessed." As Dan Bain, "Manitoba's Greatest Athlete," later recalled: "Those were the days of real athletes. When we passed, the puck never left the ice, and if the wingman wasn't there to receive it, it was because he had a broken leg."

Right: *Bain's 1901 Stanley Cup pin.*

Facing Page: *Craftsmen inscribed these souvenir sticks, circa 1899 with the particulars of Bain and his teammates' defeat at the hands of the Montreal Victorias. Their 1901 victory over the Montreal Shamrocks is recorded on this souvenir game puck. Bain's senior hockey trophy, circa 1895–1902, speedskates, circa 1905–1910, and walking cane are joined by telegrams sent during the 1901 Stanley Cup play-offs.*

Dickie Boon

Dickie Boon was born in 1878 to a prominent Montreal pioneer family whose estate would later become the site of Windsor Station. Boon began his athletic career as a speedskater, and his mercurial swiftness and extraordinary stamina would ensure his fame as captain of the 1902 Stanley Cup challengers, the Montreal Amateur Athletic Association or AAA's.

At the turn of the century—as now—substantial weight and size were considered necessary if players wished to escape being flattened into oblivion in the rough world of hockey. Blond, wiry Dickie Boon, who never weighed more than 118 pounds, used speed as his saving grace—roaring by burly, lumbering opponents whose body checks were always a few seconds behind him. The Montreal AAA's of 1902 were physically much like defenceman Dickie Boon, and most observers thought the hefty Winnipeg Victorias would steamroll their way over the AAA's for the Stanley Cup. Game One certainly seemed to bear that out: Montreal's fast little forwards couldn't get their engines going and Winnipeg took it 1–0. But Montreal sped back to whip the Victorias 5–0 in Game Two.

In the third and final game, Tom Hooper and Jack Marshall scored for Montreal in the first 11 minutes, and the defence, led by Dickie Boon, then steeled itself against the 49-minute Winnipeg onslaught that followed. The big Winnipeg forwards relentlessly attacked, and the little Montreal team just as relentlessly held them off. This so impressed *Montreal Star* sports editor Peter Spanjaardt, who was furiously telegraphing his rinkside report back to Montreal, that he said the AAA's were playing like "little men of iron." And so was coined one of hockey's most illustrious nicknames, as Dickie Boon and his "Little Men of Iron" went on to defeat Winnipeg 2–1 and win the Stanley Cup.

Right: Champions of the Canadian Amateur Hockey League (1899 to 1905) were awarded the Dewars Shield. Boon and his AAA's won the Shield and the Stanley Cup in 1902.

Facing Page: Using speed to his advantage, Captain Dickie Boon laced up these skates while starring with the Montreal AAA's circa 1900.

Joe Hall

A 1914 newspaper, which regularly published a "Dark Thought for the Day," once offered this gloomy rumination: "Suppose you had to play hockey against Joe Hall?" Beneath this ran an imaginary interview, beginning: "Joe Hall was carving a few more notches in the handle of his hockey stick…'Slip in kid, slip in,' quoth the Genial Joe, 'for I have added a few more scalps to my collection."

Yet "Bad Man" Joe Hall, the Quebec Bulldogs' rough-and-tumble defenceman, deeply regretted his violent outbursts and used to lament that he was "giving a dog a bad name."

Still, while roughing up opponents for the Bulldogs, Hall developed a nasty feud with Montreal Canadiens quicksilver winger Newsy Lalonde. After handing Lalonde a pasting during one game, Hall was later mortified to learn that Lalonde's wife had delivered a daughter that morning. A contrite Bad Joe showed up in the Canadiens dressing room after the game and begged Lalonde to let him go along to the hospital. Lalonde consented, Hall went, and there he apologized to Madame Lalonde for cutting up the father of her daughter.

When Hall was traded to the Canadiens in 1917, a managerial wit thought it would be amusing to make Hall and Lalonde roommates. The two former enemies were to become the best of friends, although their friendship was unfortunately brief. The following year would be Hall's last.

Joe Hall's contract for that 1918–19 season paid him $600 with a $100 bonus, as well as a $100 tip for a first-place finish. But Hall never got a chance to spend his $800. He and several Canadiens fell ill with Spanish influenza during Game Five of the Stanley Cup final in Seattle, and Joe Hall died in hospital on April 5, 1919, aged 36. The Stanley Cup series—tied at two wins apiece and one draw—was abandoned, the first and only time in NHL history.

Right: Eastern Canada Amateur Hockey Association schedule from 1907–08, when Joe Hall was rocking opponents as a defenceman for Montreal's AAA's and Shamrocks.

Facing Page: Resting alongside "Bad Man" Joe Hall's portrait are Quebec Bulldogs championship ribbons, circa 1912–13, Montreal Wanderers team pennant, circa 1909–1910, and the silver cup presented to Hall after he and the Kenora Thistles won the Stanley Cup in 1907.

Newsy Lalonde

Edouard "Newsy" Lalonde, a riotous and brilliant goal scorer who once potted nine goals in a game, earned his nickname as a reporter and printer for the *Cornwall Free Press*. In 1907, Sault Ste. Marie of the International League sprung Newsy from the printworks and into the pro leagues. Their $35-a-week offer reached Lalonde by telegram, along with $16 to cover the cost of a one-way ticket to "The Soo." Lalonde withdrew his last $16 in case he had to come back, and, without a penny for food, or even equipment, boarded the train south. The hungry, skateless Lalonde merely expected to watch from the sidelines, yet 20 minutes into the first game, "Soo" star Marty Walsh broke his leg and Lalonde was loaned a pair of skates. "I went all right for a while and then I got jammed into the fence. It hurt and I didn't feel good." Lalonde had to tough it out: there were no substitutes left on the bench.

A famished, wounded Lalonde took a big, restorative swig from a bottle handed to him by local boxer Jack Hammond. "It burned my mouth and my gums and my throat. I thought I was a goner." It turned out Hammond had two bottles—one of whisky and one of ammonia, used to revive fallen boxers. In the haste of the moment he had handed Lalonde the wrong bottle and Newsy had belted back an unhealthy draught of ammonia.

Lalonde recovered to score two goals, and his impressed American opponents offered him $50 a week. His Canadian club quickly matched the amount and Newsy stayed with them, thus beginning his 30-year, well-travelled career, during which he would play for Toronto, Woodstock, "The Soo," Renfrew, Vancouver, the Montreal Canadiens, Saskatoon and the New York Americans. He would win the Stanley Cup, capture the scoring championship five times in three different leagues, and come to be regarded as one of hockey's dominant players in the first half of the 20th century.

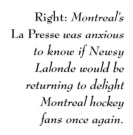

Right: Montreal's
La Presse was anxious
to know if Newsy
Lalonde would be
returning to delight
Montreal hockey
fans once again.

Facing Page:
The original "Flying
Frenchman," Lalonde
hung up these CCM
handmade skates for
good in 1926.
Original 1912 NHL
contract and inaugural
NHA schedule join
Lalonde's 1912
Vancouver PCHA
contract and
1910–11 Imperial
Tobacco watercolour
trading card.

Contract

ADOPTED BY THE

National Hockey Association of Cana

LIMIT

made this *9th* day

1912

the first part a

Hockey
Fixtures

1910-11

National Hockey
Association
of Canada

to

Lalonde

Vancouver Arena Company, Limited,

Frank A. Patrick.
MANAG'G

signed notary

and practising in

NEWSY LALONDE of RENFREW

Percy LeSueur

"Peerless Percy's" rise to become one of the great goaltenders of his time began in the Stanley Cup final of 1906. LeSueur, playing goal for Smith's Falls in a losing cause against Ottawa on March 8, greatly impressed his opponents, so much so that six days later, after Ottawa found themselves on the wrong end of a 9–1 upset in Game One of the Stanley Cup final, they hastily summoned LeSueur's netminding talents for Game Two against the Wanderers of Montreal.

A boisterous crowd of 5,000 turned up for the rematch in Ottawa, including the governor general and his wife, Earl and Lady Grey, and special trains from Montreal transported Wanderers fans to the rink.

The graceful, agile LeSueur let in an early goal, then shut down the Wanderers until his teammates had opened up a 9–1 lead. Since "total goals" in a series and not "games won" decided who would take home the Stanley Cup, Ottawa's fans were ecstatic. Their Silver Seven had done the impossible: they had tied the total score 10–10. The Wanderers notched their play up a level, and Lester Patrick potted two late, desperate goals to give Montreal the Stanley Cup. But LeSueur's star had been established. He became captain of the Senators and backstopped the team to two Stanley Cups in 1909 and 1911.

After serving with the 48th Highlanders in World War I, LeSueur resumed what would be a 50-year career in professional hockey, moving from goaling to refereeing, then to coaching as the Detroit Olympias' first bench boss. The cerebral LeSueur also invented the gauntlet-type glove for goalies, as well as the goal net used by the NHA and the NHL from 1912–25. He was also an accomplished columnist and broadcaster and an original member of *Hockey Night in Canada's* "Hot Stove League," chronicling for a new generation of fans the hockey exploits of a new generation of legends.

Right: Ticket to the Stanley Cup series in which LeSueur launched his career.

Facing Page: From 1905 to 1910, LeSueur wielded this battered "goaler" stick, winning the Stanley Cup along the way in 1909. The 1910 pennant celebrated Ottawa's NHA entry, which coincided with an Imperial Tobacco trading card series, 1910–11. This card features LeSueur in a beautiful water-colour rendering.

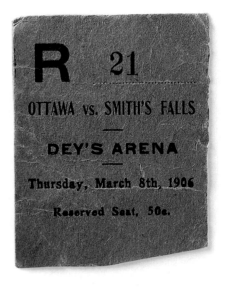

R 21

OTTAWA vs. SMITH'S FALLS

—

DEY'S ARENA

Thursday, March 8th, 1906

Reserved Seat, 50c.

John Ambrose O'Brien

The Godfather of Professional Hockey—the man responsible for the Montreal Canadiens and expansion to the Pacific coast as well as hockey's improved organization and salary structure—would have been just another obscure millionaire sportsman had the Eastern Canada Hockey Association said "yes" to him in 1909. The powerful hockey team from O'Brien's hometown of Renfrew, Ontario, had grown weary of mopping up the Ottawa Valley's amateur senior league so they asked the 24-year-old O'Brien to state their case in Montreal to join the pros. The ECHA said "no," and at the same meeting expelled the Montreal Wanderers. A fuming O'Brien, assisted by an equally disgruntled Wanderers management, went on to organize the National Hockey Association—the immediate forerunner of the National Hockey League.

O'Brien's wealthy father, who had made a fortune in railway building and mining, put up the money for four of the NHA's first five franchises: Renfrew, Cobalt (whose players all worked in the silver mine and were once paid in nuggets), Haileybury and the Montreal Canadiens, with the understanding that control of the latter would promptly be assumed by francophone sportsmen in Montreal. John O'Brien's compelling desire was the Stanley Cup for Renfrew, and so he bought the talent to win it with then staggering largesse: $3,000 each to the innovative Patrick brothers, whose experiences in the NHA would help them form the PCHA in 1911; $3,000 and $5,200 to goal-scoring aces Marty Walsh and Cyclone Taylor over two seasons; and $2,000 to the bulletlike shooter Fred Whitcroft. Because of their whopping payroll, the team immediately became known as the Millionaires but couldn't make any money themselves because of their small rink. They also couldn't win a Stanley Cup, for as John O'Brien later explained: "We had too many highly paid stars on one team." When the NHA folded in 1917, John O'Brien went back to managing the family businesses, leaving a hockey legacy as rich as the gold in the O'Brien mines.

Art Ross

Art Ross was born the 12th of 13 children to the chief factor of a Hudson Bay fur trading post in Northern Ontario. One of hockey's great players and inventors, Ross grew up speaking fluent Ojibway and learned to skate on Whitefish Bay using primitive clamp-on skates. Ross turned pro in 1906 with the Kenora Thistles and helped defeat the Montreal Wanderers for the Stanley Cup in January 1907. He then bounced to the Wanderers, to the Haileybury Comets, back to Montreal, and then to the Ottawa Senators, where the Wanderers' speedy goal scorer Harry Hyland said Ross played like "an eel. He was one of the greatest stickhandlers I ever saw. He could spin on a dime... and he was so tricky there was no blocking him."

It was while Ottawa was travelling to Montreal for the 1915 NHA championship that Ross invented "kitty-bar-the-door" hockey, thinking that the fast, powerful Wanderers could be stopped by stringing three defencemen across the width of the ice, 30 feet in front of the goalie, defying any Montreal forward to skate through. The confident Wanderers, playing on home ice, even had a fleet of taxis waiting outside the rink to take them to the railway station so they could head west to meet Vancouver for the Stanley Cup. Their pride and Art Ross's defensive shell ensured the taxis came in handy for the Ottawa Senators, who won the round on goals and caught the train to the coast.

Art Ross went on to invent the B-shaped, puck-trapping goal net; made the puck truer, faster and safer by bevelling the edge; perfected a protective device for vulnerable Achilles tendons; and developed the Art Ross helmet. He also became a referee and three-time Stanley Cup winner as coach and general manager of the Boston Bruins. To commemorate his rich strategic and innovative legacy, the fur trader's son is remembered by the Art Ross Trophy, awarded annually to the National Hockey League's premier scorer.

Right: Schedule from the NHA's inaugural 1910–11 season, when the Haileybury Comets featured the legendary Art Ross on defence.

Facing Page: Ross signed this 1910 contract for a tidy sum of $2,700 and agreed to play 10 weeks plus play-offs for the Haileybury Comets. That same year, Imperial Tobacco selected Ross for their 1910–11 watercolour trading card series. Ross donned the Montreal Wanderers' colours for eight seasons between 1908 and 1918.

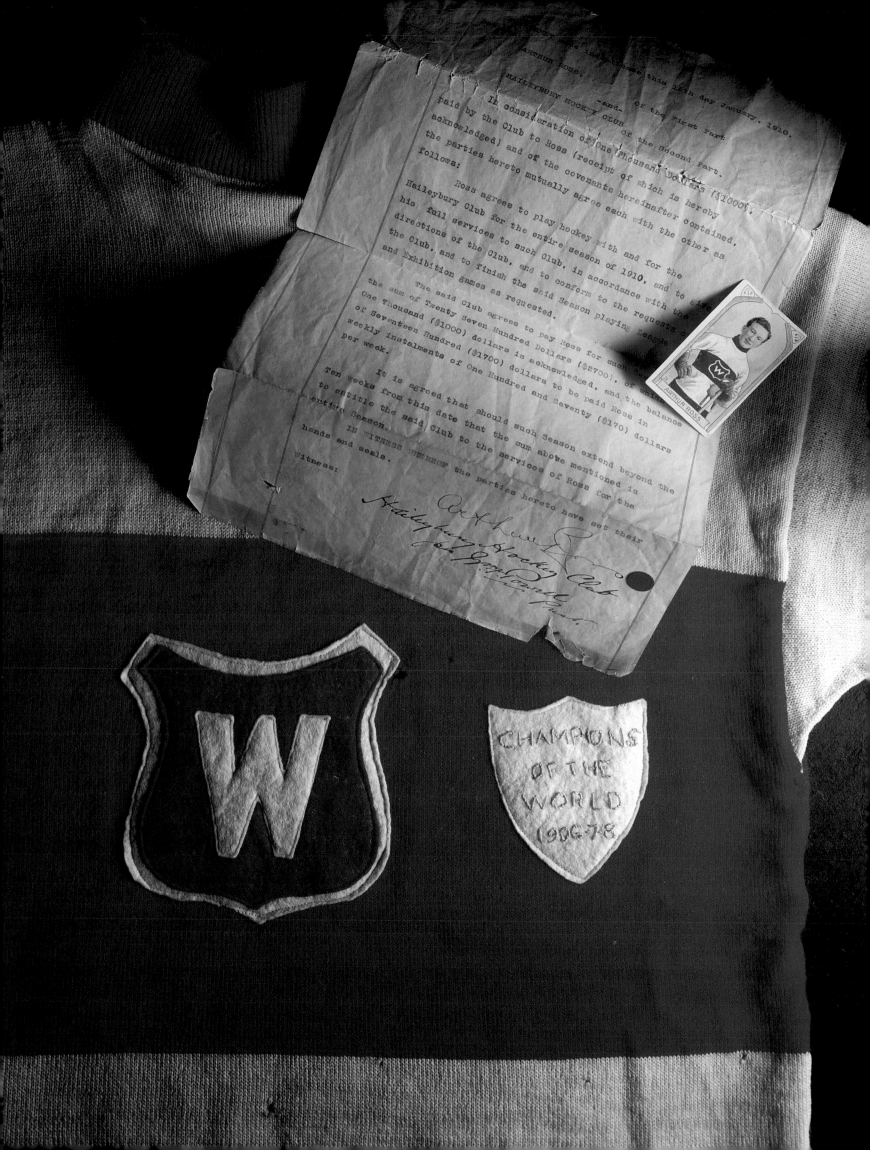

Cyclone Taylor

Frederick "Cyclone" Taylor, hockey's first true superstar, was a man whose sporting prowess was so spectacular it has become legendary. After watching Taylor score four dazzling goals for Ottawa on January 11, 1908, Canada's Governor General Earl Grey enthused within earshot of a reporter that Taylor was "a cyclone if ever I saw one." The next edition of the *Ottawa Free Press* announced: "In Portage la Prairie they called him a tornado, in Houghton, Michigan, he was known as a whirlwind. From now on he'll be known as Cyclone Taylor."

When Taylor left Ottawa for the Renfrew Millionaires and the breathtaking sum of $5,200—more than the salary of Prime Minister Wilfred Laurier, more than any Canadian athlete had ever been paid—Ottawa fans howled at this unspeakable betrayal by the man who had led them to the Stanley Cup the year before. They hurled empty whisky bottles and frozen "horse apples" at Taylor as Ottawa defeated Renfrew 8–5 on February 12, 1910.

Gentlemanly Taylor vowed revenge, promising that in the next meeting between Ottawa and Renfrew—the last of the season—he would score a goal while skating backwards.

As the *Renfrew Journal* reported on March 10, 1910: "Taylor got the puck on a pass and skating down in his usual fine fashion, he turned, and going backwards, he skated a piece and then sent the shot home to the Ottawa nets with skill and swiftness." Taylor's desire to get even with Ottawa led Renfrew to a humiliating 17–2 victory over the demoralized Senators.

Cyclone Taylor then went west to star with the Vancouver Millionaires, leading them to the Stanley Cup in 1915, and once again becoming the most famous man in Canada. The Cyclone lived to the great age of 93 and was often asked about his "backwards" goal. But he never confirmed nor denied it. True to his wry style, he once gently admonished a brash sportswriter by reminding him that "so many different versions have been written by writers who are my friends that I don't want to spoil anybody's story."

Right: *"The Most Excellent Order of the British Empire" was awarded to Taylor for his services during World War II.*

Facing Page: *Cyclone's "Ottawa" game stick, circa 1908, shows the wear of his two seasons as a defenceman playing 21 games, scoring 17 goals and winning the Stanley Cup in 1909. Taylor would win the Cup again in 1915 with the Vancouver Millionaires, where he was presented with this "World Champions 1915" gold medal.*

*S*ince man first propelled himself over the frozen waterways and byways of winter, the skate has evolved from crudely sculpted bone fragments used in medieval times to the gleaming steel, moulded plastic and superbly fashioned leather boot of today's precise instrument. Throughout the skate's evolutionary process, the objective has been consistent—to transport the skater across his chosen arena, faster and with greater comfort. Pictured from left to right, top row: (above and below) two styles of early wooden European skates with steel blades, circa 1820; skate runner which attached to a boot, circa 1850; skate with harness for boot, circa 1880. Second row: skate with boot, straight flat blade, circa 1910; tube skate, circa 1920; Starr skates, circa 1920. Third row: Frank Foyston's flat-bladed leather skate, circa 1928; tube skate with added support in ankles, circa 1940. Fourth row: Gordie Howe's leather skate, with tube blade and high ankle support, circa 1965; moulded plastic skate with plastic protection on blade, circa 1975. Fifth row: leather skate, tube blade, high tongue, circa 1965; Harry Howell's leather skate, tube blade with protection on butt, circa 1973; and leather skate with plastic protection on blade, protected toe and high tongue, circa 1990.

1917 1926

Birth of the NHL

Ontario senior
championship pin,
circa 1920.
Left: Original NHL
minute book, schedule,
program, seal, contract
and Windsor Hotel card.

"At a meeting of representatives of hockey
clubs held at the Windsor Hotel, Montreal,
November 22nd, 1917, the following present
G. W. Kendall, S. E. Lichtenhein, F. R. Gorman,
M. J. Quinn and Frank Calder, it was explained by the last named
that in view of the suspension of operations by the National
Hockey Association of Canada Limited, he had called the meeting
at the suggestion of the Quebec Hockey Club to ascertain if
some steps could not be taken to perpetuate the game of hockey."

Thus reads the first item of business on the first page of the

Frank Calder

The National Hockey League's first president and guiding light until 1943 came to Canada from Bristol, England, as a 23-year-old schoolteacher in 1900. A passionate cricketer and soccer player, Calder soon moved into journalism, becoming a crusading Montreal sportswriter.

Calder published one of the first attacks on professional wrestling, suggesting that Montreal's influential promoter George Kennedy was part of a trust that was fixing matches. Kennedy was not amused but said, "You've got to admit the guy has plenty of guts to write it." It was that kind of principled fortitude that Kennedy admired a few years later when, as owner of the Montreal Canadiens, he lobbied to have Calder elected to the National Hockey Association's executive and later to the presidency of the NHL, where Calder served with distinction for 26 years. He is commemorated by the Calder Trophy, which he instituted in the 1936-37 season as the award to the NHL's top rookie.

The romance of hockey's bygone era, captured on this school notebook cover, circa 1920.

Frank Calder Memorial Trophy, established by the NHL in 1943, continues the tradition of honouring the NHL's most outstanding rookie.

first National Hockey League Minute Book, a purple-and-ochre tome chronicling the affairs of the league expressly formed to "perpetuate the game of hockey." In all likelihood, however, it was formed to squeeze out fractious Toronto Arenas former owner Eddie Livingstone, whose belligerent nature had made life difficult for the other teams in the now defunct NHA.

After transplanted British schoolteacher and sportswriter Frank Calder was elected Chair of the meeting, a discussion followed resulting in the motion "that the Canadiens, Wanderers, Ottawa, and Quebec Hockey Clubs unite to comprise the National Hockey League." The motion was carried, and just as the gathered were moving on to other business, W. E. Northey, representing the new owners of the Toronto Arenas, asked and received permission to enter the meeting. Northey had been dispatched to say that in the event of a four-team league being formed, the Livingstone-free Toronto Arenas wished to be included. Quebec's representative, M. J. Quinn, ventured the financially troubled Bulldogs would be willing to suspend operations provided they could sell their players to other teams.

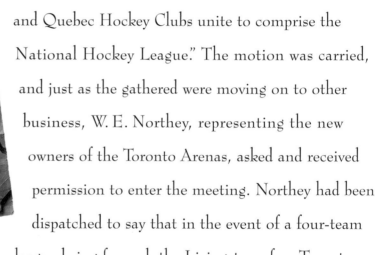

After discussion it was unanimously agreed that the Quebec players would be taken over by the league at a cost of $700 each. The Montreal Canadiens acquired Billy Mummery and future Hall of Famers Joe Malone and Joe Hall, while Quebec's remaining players were dispersed throughout the league—which now included the Toronto Arenas.

Frank Calder was elected president and secretary-treasurer at a salary of $800 on the understanding that there could be no appeal of his decisions. A schedule was drawn up, and the meeting was then adjourned. In the corridor outside the meeting, the *Montreal Herald's* young sports reporter Elmer Ferguson rushed up to the first man to emerge, who happened to be Frank Calder, and begged to know what happened. "Not too much, Fergie," Calder replied, before stepping onto an elevator and into hockey history. The National Hockey League was born.

The first NHL games were played December 19, 1917. The Montreal Canadiens won their opener over Ottawa 7–4, with future NHL scoring champ Joe Malone firing in five goals. The Montreal Wanderers edged Toronto in a 10–9 thriller, played before only 700 fans even though soldiers were admitted free as the Arenas' guests. The Toronto team must have shuddered at this inauspicious beginning, for they were now governed by the iron fist of Charlie Querrie, who posted for their edification the following rules in the Toronto dressing room:

1. First and foremost, do not forget that I am running this club. 2. You are being paid to give your best services to the club. Condition depends a lot on how you behave off the ice. 3. It does not require bravery to hit another man over the head with a stick. If you want to fight, go over to France.

Querrie went on to remind the team that if they didn't want "to be on the square and play hockey" they could turn in their uniforms and go look for work elsewhere. Which Querrie himself soon did, citing interference from none other than Eddie Livingstone, the man the NHL had been formed to exclude.

From 1917 to 1926, the NHL would grow into a 10-team international league and see the debut of the likes of Howie Morenz,

"Babe" Dye's photo trading card, circa 1923–24.

Cecil "Babe" Dye

Cecil Dye was a gifted all-round athlete, powering football's Toronto Argonauts at halfback and having such a golden glove that baseball legend Connie Mack of the Philadelphia Athletics offered The Babe the small fortune of $25,000 to come south to play America's game. Yet Babe Dye chose hockey, and, not being modest with details of his other athletic achievements, did not at first endear himself to the management of the Toronto St. Pats, who played him as a substitute right-winger in the 1919–20 season. Cracking the regular lineup the following year, The Babe led the league in scoring, potting 35 goals in 24 games and managing to score in 11 consecutive contests. Dye would repeat both feats the following year and lead the St. Pats to the Stanley Cup by scoring 11 goals in seven games. Though not a dazzling skater, the five-foot-eight-inch, 150-pound Dye was a magical stickhandler and possessed a booming shot comparable to that of Didier "Cannonball" Pitre. With Jack Adams as his centre, Dye would twice more lead the league in scoring in 1923 and 1925. Dye was sold to Chicago after the 1926 season, and, after breaking his leg in the 1927 training camp, he lost his scoring touch, tallying only one goal in the 59 games he played until his 1931 retirement.

Hamilton Tigers NHL Hockey Club corporate seal, circa 1920.

Cooper Smeaton

"A referee is always paid and receives the same salary regardless what team wins," said Cooper Smeaton. But a small group of vocal and abusive Ottawa fans thought Smeaton more than a touch blind to the sins of the opposition. Smeaton, who would win the Military Medal in World War I for tossing crates of ammunition off a burning truck as shell fire rained down around him, showed the same equanimity when barraged by the merciless invective of four Ottawa fans. The only time his tormentors succeeded in catching his attention was the night they hopped the boards just before game time and handed the bemused referee two silver loving cups, along with a note: "As you are well aware, during the season of 1916 you have received considerable criticism from…the patrons of "Murderers Row"…We, accordingly, take this opportunity of handing you this small pair of cups to show that even we, who know it all, appreciate the fact that you too are conversant with at least a portion of the rules of the National Hockey Association. Incidentally, we hope to see you with us during the season of 1917 because a new [referee] might not accept, with the same good grace, the verbal abuse we have handed you this winter."

Official score card from an exhibition tournament in Winnipeg.

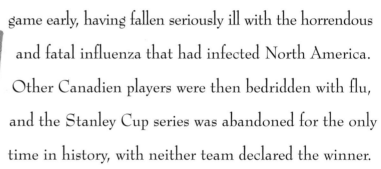

Silver cups awarded to Smeaton by the patrons of "Murderers Row."

King Clancy, Nels Stewart, Frank Boucher, Eddie Shore, Bill and Bun Cook, "Tiny" Thompson and Aurèle Joliat.

Rule changes, many invented by the Patrick brothers, were implemented. Goalies, for example, were allowed to adopt any position to block shots. Previously, netminders had been required to stand up to keep the puck out of the net and could be penalized for flopping or falling.

The first NHL-PCHA Stanley Cup game on the West Coast was played in 1919 between the Seattle Metropolitans and the Montreal Canadiens. The teams each had two wins and were tied when Game Five was called after one hour and 40 minutes of overtime. Montreal's Joe Hall left the game early, having fallen seriously ill with the horrendous and fatal influenza that had infected North America. Other Canadien players were then bedridden with flu, and the Stanley Cup series was abandoned for the only time in history, with neither team declared the winner.

Hall of Famer Cecil "Babe" Dye entered the NHL in 1920 with the former Toronto Arenas, now renamed the St. Patricks in the hope that the luck of the Irish would go with them. Dye won the league scoring title in 1921 with 35 goals in 24 games. He won the scoring title again the following year (and twice more), leading the St. Pats to the 1922 Stanley Cup. He was also awarded the first penalty shot in Stanley Cup play during that series, and The Babe, a touch rattled by the formality of it all, let fly with a shot that missed by "36 feet."

In March of 1923, Foster Hewitt, a 21-year-old cub reporter with the Toronto Star's radio station, was surprised by an assignment to broadcast one of radio's first hockey games, an intermediate amateur play-off contest between Kitchener and Toronto Parkdale played at Toronto's Mutual

Street Arena. He discharged his duties so well that his boss put hockey broadcasts on Hewitt's beat, and a national tradition was launched.

The new league grew confident that it would last and began to expand. In 1924, the first NHL franchise was established in an American city with the awarding of the Bruins to Boston and owner Charles Adams, thus making the NHL "international." Former Montreal Wanderers star Art Ross was appointed manager. The Montreal Maroons entered the league in 1924 and won their first Stanley Cup two years later.

After the Hamilton Tigers staged a 1925 strike because their extended game schedule did not include more money for the extra games, they were suspended and sold to New York City, where they became the Americans. The message was clear: any attempts to flout Frank Calder's authority would not be tolerated.

Yet the National Hockey League was by no means the only game in town. The Western Canada Hockey League (formed in 1921 with teams in Alberta and Saskatchewan) competed with the Pacific Coast Hockey Association and the NHL for the Stanley Cup. By the mid-1920s, however, the other leagues were running into financial trouble and folding, finding then—as today—that though a small market might have a ravenous appetite for hockey, it couldn't support the game at the gate. In 1926, when the Montreal Canadiens beat the previous year's Stanley Cup champions, the Victoria Cougars of the Western Hockey League, it marked the last time a team outside the NHL would challenge for Lord Stanley's trophy. By the end of the 1925–26 season, with the demise of the once illustrious Western Hockey League, the NHL had become the dominant hockey conglomerate, and the Stanley Cup its sole dominion.

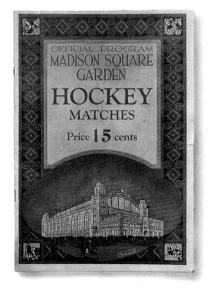

Program commemorating Madison Square Garden's inaugural season. 1925–26.

Lady Byng Memorial Trophy honouring sportsmanship and hockey excellence.

Madison Square Garden

When colourful New York boxing promoter George "Tex" Rickard discovered in 1924 that the old Madison Square Garden was to be razed to make way for a skyscraper, he assembled a team of businessmen he called his "600 millionaires," set up financing, and broke ground for a new Madison Square Garden on January 9, 1925. After travelling to Montreal with Damon Runyon to watch the flamboyantly talented Howie Morenz and his Montreal Canadiens raise the game of ice hockey to the sublime, Rickard was convinced New Yorkers would embrace the fast, rugged sport and installed ice in his new building. He rented the rink to the New York Americans for a season and, after seeing their popularity swell, realized New York could support two teams and hired young Conn Smythe to create a rival to the Americans. On November 17, 1926, the New York Rangers won their first game in the Garden by defeating the Montreal Maroons 1–0, and another hockey dynasty was born.

Harry Cameron's pocket watch.

Harry Cameron

Defenceman Harry Cameron, whose riotous temperament often gave him grief in the form of fines and suspensions, scored more goals than any other defender in Stanley Cup competition until 1926. Just as notable, he won his three Stanley Cups playing for three different Toronto teams: the Blueshirts of 1914, the Arenas of 1918 and the St. Patricks of 1922. Though only 154 pounds, Cameron pounded much larger opponents and fired 171 goals into the nets in his 312-game, 14-year career. Hockey historians suggest that the remarkable Cameron was also the first man to curve his shot without curving his stick, instead spinning the puck by laterally sliding the stick as he shot.

Albert "Babe" Siebert

Babe Siebert starred in the Ontario Hockey Association as a junior before bulldozing into the NHL with the Montreal Maroons in the 1925–26 season as a rawboned 21-year-old. Siebert, played on a Stanley Cup winner in his first year in the big leagues, and his aggressive play earned him a formidable 116 minutes in penalties. Maroons coach Eddie Gerrard saw "defenceman" written all over The Babe and put him on the blue line until 1930. Siebert was then moved up front, dazzling at left wing on the Maroons "S" line alongside Hooley Smith and Nels Stewart. The trio tore up the NHL and when not potting goals managed to compile more than 200 minutes in penalties for their three seasons together. In 1933, Siebert was sold to the New York Rangers, where Lester Patrick paired him on defence with Ching Johnson as the Rangers went on to win the Stanley Cup.

Another trade sent The Babe to Boston before one brought him back to Montreal to don the Canadiens' colours. There he would win the Hart Trophy in 1937 as the NHL's most valuable player.

Program from "Babe" Siebert's rookie season with the Montreal Maroons.

The First NHL Strike

In the spring of 1925, the NHL's first-place Hamilton Tigers mutinied when they discovered they had played 30 games but their contracts–and compensation–were only for 24. The Tigers wanted $200 a man to play the winner of the Canadiens vs. Toronto series for the league championship. Until then, they were on strike.

The NHL and President Frank Calder were unyielding. At a special meeting of the league, this fifth item of business was recorded: "The situation

Table hockey game, circa 1920, reflects the fact that blue and red lines had not yet been introduced.

arising out of a "strike" of players of the Hamilton Club in the play-off series was discussed when it was moved by Mr. Dandurand seconded by Mr. Querrie that the fine and suspension imposed on the players of the Hamilton Club be confirmed and that the future of the players be left in the hands of the President."

On April 17, Calder suspended the Hamilton players indefinitely and fined them the sum they had requested to continue playing: $200 each. The NHL announced that the Hamilton franchise would move to New York the following season, and the third-place Montreal Canadiens eventually became the Stanley Cup champs of 1925.

Prince of Wales Trophy

In 1924, devoted sportsman H.R.H. the Prince of Wales donated a hockey trophy bearing his name, one which has gone through many incarnations as the league has remodelled itself over the years. The Prince of Wales Trophy was first awarded to the champions of the NHL who would then go on to compete with the Western Canada Hockey League winners for the Stanley Cup. With the demise of the WHL in 1926, the trophy became the award for the first-place finishers of the NHL's American Division. The NHL returned to one all-encompassing division in 1938, and the trophy once again went to the winners of the NHL championship. Expansion in 1967 saw the Prince of Wales Trophy going to the East Division champs until 1973–74, then to the regular season winner of the newly created Prince of Wales Conference until 1981–82, when it was awarded to the play-off winners of the conference that shared the trophy's name.

Prince of Wales Trophy.

Cy Denneny wore this skate as he led the NHL in scoring in 1923-24.

Cy Denneny

Short, stocky Cy Denneny looked more like a bouncer than a talented goal scorer, but in fact he was both. After joining the Ottawa Senators in 1916, the left-winger kept opponents from pushing around his sweet-natured linemates Frank Nighbor and Jack Darragh. And when later paired with right-winger Punch Broadbent, the duo became known as "The Gold Dust Twins," such was their sparkling élan at keeping opponents honest and on guard.

Denneny stayed with the Senators until 1928, firing in more goals than any other Ottawa player and never dropping below fourth in the league scoring totals in 10 years. The frequently battered Denneny won five Stanley Cups in his career, and potted the winning goal in overtime at the 1923 Stanley Cup final against Edmonton. Cy Denneny led the league in scoring in 1923 and

added to his fame by falling down a farmer's well after impatiently leaving a snowbound train during a road trip. Only his pride was hurt.

Joe Malone

Gentlemanly, stylish, "Phantom" Joe Malone played seven illustrious and prolific seasons with the Quebec Bulldogs, two with the Montreal Canadiens, and two with the Hamilton Tigers, where he was also coach and manager.

Malone, a flashy stickhandler and slick skater, was a relentless goal scorer, achieving three or more goals in 47 games over his 16-year pro career. On January 31, 1920, Malone scored seven goals for Quebec against the Toronto St. Pats, netting three of them within 120 seconds. Three weeks later he scored his fourth goal and the game winner against Montreal in overtime, and on March 10, potted six against Ottawa. Over the course of his seven-year NHL tour, the Quebec City native racked up 146 goals in 125 regular season games, leading the league in 1917–18 with an astonishing 44 goals in 20 games. ●

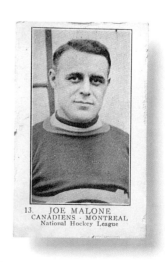

"Phantom" Joe Malone photo trading card, circa 1923–24.

Frank Foyston

Frank Foyston's brilliant hockey career spanned five leagues and most of North America, and included some of the significant firsts of hockey's early years. After playing centre for the Eaton's Company team in Toronto, which won the 1911 Ontario Hockey Association title, Foyston turned pro with the Toronto Blueshirts of the NHA in 1912–13 and centred a line with Hall of Famers Allan "Scotty" Davidson and Jack Walker when the team won the Stanley Cup in 1914.

The following year, Foyston jumped to the Seattle Metropolitans of the Pacific Coast Hockey Association. Despite a choppy skating stride that made it look as if he was travelling faster than he was, Foyston won a sports-writers' poll and trophy for being the best all-round player in that league for the 1916–17 season. Bold and clever around the net, Foyston scored four goals in seven games as the Mets became the first American team to win the Stanley Cup, defeating the Montreal Canadiens in 1917.

Two years later, Foyston skated into hockey legend again by scoring nine goals in the historic 1919 Stanley Cup series before it was cancelled due to the Spanish influenza epidemic. Then, after nine seasons with the Mets, he sailed up the coast to join the Western Canada Hockey League Victoria Cougars. There he further entrenched himself in NHL lore by playing on the Stanley-Cup-winning Cougars team of 1925, the last time a non-NHL team won top prize. The Cougars were sold to Detroit in 1926, and Foyston went with them, playing until 1928 when he returned to the Pacific Northwest. The *Seattle Post-Intelligencer* placed the estimable Foyston in the sporting pantheon with these eulogistic words in 1966: "You missed one of the all-time greats if you never saw Frank Foyston perform with a hockey stick. He wielded it like Fritz Kreisler his bow, Willie Mays his bat and Arnold Palmer his two-iron."

Right: The Pacific Coast Hockey Association honoured Seattle's Frank Foyston as the league's best all-round player for 1916–17, the season the Mets became the first American team to win the Stanley Cup.

Facing Page: Battle-worn gloves and skates, circa 1928, of all-time great Frank Foyston adorn his Seattle Metropolitan game jersey, circa 1917.

Frank Frederickson

Scholar, hockey star, Olympian, aviator and musician, Frank Frederickson received his first pair of skates at age five. Yet until his father flooded their Winnipeg backyard one winter to encourage a game of ice hockey for the neighbourhood children, Frank Frederickson could only speak the Icelandic language of his immigrant parents.

Frederickson learned English well enough to land himself at the University of Manitoba, where he captained and centred the varsity ice hockey team and played violin in a dance band. World War I interrupted his idyll, so the intrepid Frederickson joined the Royal Flying Corps for a tour of duty in Egypt and won his wings. While sailing back to England, his ship was torpedoed by a German submarine, and the future scoring champ and Stanley Cup winner was left floating on a life raft in the Mediterranean for 12 hours. A Japanese ship came to the rescue, finding Frederickson clad only in his pyjamas and clutching his cherished violin.

After his star turn at the 1920 Antwerp Olympic Games with Canada's gold-medal-winning hockey team, Frederickson returned to Winnipeg to play violin in the band at the Fort Garry Hotel. Lester Patrick, however, had other plans for the young musician. He parked himself in the hotel ballroom and cajoled, wooed and finally, by requesting "Ain't We Got Fun," induced Frederickson to come west and skate for his Victoria Aristocrats.

Right: Victoria Cougars souvenir mini hockey stick commemorating Frederickson and his teammates' Stanley Cup victory.

Facing Page: Donning this Victoria Cougars jersey, star centre Frederickson notched six goals in eight games, bringing the Stanley Cup to Victoria in 1925. Frederickson went on to play, coach and manage the NHL Pittsburgh Pirates in 1928.

At the end of the 1922 season, Frederickson quit Victoria to return to Winnipeg and his love of music. He and his homesick bride, a graduate from the Toronto Conservatory, sunk their hopes and savings into "Frank Frederickson's Melody Shop." When Patrick went to retrieve his recalcitrant star, he found him running the till while his classically trained wife played popular ditties for the patrons. Patrick was undaunted: he bet Frederickson $100 that his business wouldn't last a year. Frederickson won the bet, but lost $2,400 on the business. The battle of wills was over. Frederickson returned to Victoria to the renamed Cougars to win the PCHA scoring title in 1923, and the Stanley Cup in 1925.

Harry Holmes

Along with Jack Walker and Frank Foyston, Harry "Hap" Holmes was one of the "Three Musketeers" who moved from the 1914 Stanley-Cup-winning Toronto Blueshirts to whiff Pacific breezes with the Seattle Metropolitans. A journeyman goaltender of uncommon grit, Holmes tied the illustrious Georges Vezina as the NHA's leading goaltender.

In his 15-year career, Holmes kicked out pucks in five leagues: with Toronto of the NHA; Seattle of the PCHA; Victoria of both the Western Canada Hockey League and Western Hockey League; and Toronto and Detroit of the NHL.

The man the newspapers called "nerveless" had a career goals-against average of 2.9, second only to that of Hall of Famer Clint Benedict.

Hap guarded the cage on seven championship teams and four Stanley Cup winners, but one of his most legendary feats came in the nets for Seattle during the infamous 1919 Stanley Cup finals against Montreal.

After Holmes shut out the Habs 7–0 under "seven man aside" western rules in Game One, the Montrealers retrieved their championship style in Game Two, with Newsy Lalonde potting every Canadiens goal in their 4–2 victory under "six aside" eastern rules.

Seattle struck back in Game Three, winning 7–2, and it wasn't until Game Four that the teams finally transcended the rule differences. After a brutal, scoreless 60 minutes, the match went into overtime. Both teams dredged up reserves of desire and hammered at each other's goalies, but both Vezina and Holmes stopped every puck. No substitutions were made for the first 15 minutes, and at the 20-minute mark, with the exhausted teams deadlocked, referee Mickey Ion put them out of their misery and called the game a draw. When several Canadiens players fell ill with the deadly Spanish influenza, the next game was cancelled–and so were the Stanley Cup finals.

To commemorate the endurance and skill of Hap Holmes, the American Hockey League has awarded its leading goalie the Hap Holmes Memorial Trophy since 1941.

Right: Souvenir pennant celebrating Holmes and the Toronto Blueshirts' 1914 Stanley Cup championship over the Victoria Aristocrats.

Facing Page: Resplendent in the vibrant colours of this jersey, "Hap" Holmes backstopped the Seattle Metropolitans to the first ever American Stanley Cup victory in 1917.

Aurèle Joliat

Aurèle Emile Joliat, who soared on left wing with the "Flying Frenchmen" during his 16 seasons as a Hab, was not French Canadian at all but the son of a Swiss Protestant who immigrated to Ottawa in the late 1800s.

In his black trademark cap, custom made by a Montreal tailor, the diminutive Joliat, variously known as "Mighty Mite," "Mighty Atom" and "Little Giant," drove opposing teams mad with skating, passing and stickhandling that challenged the laws of gravity. Toronto winger Babe Dye once skated over to the Montreal bench and wearily said to Habs owner Leo Dandurand: "Move Joliat to centre, Leo, hold a mirror to each side of him and you'll have the fastest line in hockey."

After smashing up his leg playing football, Joliat decided to try the more genteel sport of hockey, where he accrued six shoulder separations, three broken ribs and five broken noses during his career. While on a harvesting trip to Saskatchewan, Joliat signed with the Saskatoon Crescents, but he would soon find himself famous when Montreal sent the great veteran Newsy Lalonde to Saskatoon for the playing rights of the unknown rookie Joliat in a startling 1922 trade.

Teamed with Billy Boucher and Howie Morenz the following season, Joliat was launched as one of the greatest left-wingers in NHL history, scoring 270 NHL goals—the same number as the glorious Morenz. Yet Joliat's tenacious checking also earned him a good deal of attention, most of it unwelcome. The Montreal Maroons' Hooley Smith carried on an aggressive feud with Joliat, who finally had enough and struck back. "Just as I was chasing Smith over the boards," recalled Joliat, "this chief of police, who had a seat along the edge, grabbed me by the shoulders. I reached over and dragged him right out on the ice, and tore his coon-coat right off his back. Only fight I ever won." Joliat would also win three Stanley Cups with the Canadiens, and a reputation as the greatest left wing of his era.

Right: Colourful hand-tooled leather wallet belonging to Montreal Canadiens' flamboyant star Aurèle Joliat.

Facing Page: Four-time NHL All-Star Joliat was a distinctive figure dashing down the left wing with his trademark black cap, shown here with his Champ's Cigarettes photo trading card, circa 1924–25. Joliat's silverware included three Stanley Cups and the Hart Trophy. This personal collection includes a variety of trophies from adoring fans, media and corporate well-wishers.

Frank Nighbor

The "Pembroke Peach," renowned for his poke check, was one of the greatest two-way centres in the history of the game. Hockey reporter Baz O'Meara, once explained why: "The continual and sometimes brutal attack by less skilled forwards…made him switch his play from offensive to defensive," just for self-preservation.

Nighbor was thought to be too small for big-time hockey, and it was only when his boyhood friend Harry Cameron refused to report to Port Arthur unless Nighbor was signed too that "The Flying Dutchman" was given his chance. In his first game he scored six goals and would never warm the bench again.

Nighbor won his first Stanley Cup with the 1915 Vancouver Millionaires, then returned to his beloved Ottawa to become a stalwart for the Senators, with whom he would win four more Stanley Cups.

In 1923, Dr. David Hart, father of former Montreal Canadiens manager Cecil Hart, donated what has become one of hockey's most cherished individual awards, a trophy recognizing the player judged most valuable to his team. Nighbor was the first winner of the Hart Trophy, and the following year, the courteous and civilized Nighbor was invited to Rideau Hall by Lady Byng, a fervent hockey fan. A nervous Nighbor arrived at the stroke of eight, whereupon the governor general's wife put him at ease by showing him a huge trophy and asking whether he thought the NHL would be inclined to accept it as a token of her love of the game. Nighbor replied that the league would be delighted, as was Lady Byng, who handed him the cup, saying, "I present this trophy to Frank Nighbor as the most sportsmanlike player of 1925." An astonished Nighbor graciously accepted the award, sent Lady Byng a basket of roses, and went on to win Lady Byng's legacy the following year, as well as one more Stanley Cup in 1927.

Right: Ottawa program, circa 1929, featuring the Senators' legendary Frank Nighbor, the first winner of the illustrious Hart and Lady Byng trophies.

Facing Page: Nighbor's timeworn skates, circa 1923, carried him to stardom with the Ottawa Senators, where he wore their team colours for 15 years. A striking figure, "Dutch" was often in the spotlight, as shown in this Champ's Cigarettes 1924–25 trading card.

WORLDS
CHAMPIONS
1922-23

FRANK J. NIGHBOR

Georges Vezina

"The Chicoutimi Cucumber," renowned for his coolness under fire, was one of the game's greatest goaltenders. Yet he didn't learn to skate until he was 18. Instead, he played goal in his boots, an accepted practice at the turn of the century.

Vezina was discovered in 1910 during a barnstorming match between Chicoutimi and the Montreal Canadiens. Vezina and his team of amateurs shut out the Habs, so impressing Montreal goalie Joseph Cattarinich that he persuaded Canadiens' owner George Kennedy to sign up Vezina, even though it would mean the end of Cattarinich's job. The Cucumber would go on to play 328 league games and 39 more in the play-offs—all for the Habs.

On November 28, 1925, after never missing a game in his 15-year pro career, Vezina pulled himself out of net in a game against Pittsburgh, suffering from chest pains and dizziness. He was diagnosed with tuberculosis and left without saying good-bye, hoping one day to return to the game he loved.

As Canadiens' owner Leo Dandurand recalled in the *Montreal Star*, Vezina did return in late March of 1926, scrawny and wheezing, his lungs ravaged. Vezina, a man familiar with sorrow having seen 22 of his 24 children die in infancy, turned up in the Canadiens dressing room at his customary game-day time and settled in his usual corner. Dandurand "glanced at him as he sat there, and saw tears rolling down his cheeks. He was looking at his old pads and skates that [trainer] Eddie Dufour had arranged in Georges' corner, thinking he would don them that night. Then he asked one little favour—the sweater he wore in the last world series. Then he went." Vezina died on March 24, 1926, and the next year Canadiens' owners Leo Dandurand, Leo Letourneau and Joseph Cattarinich—the man who had discovered Vezina 15 years earlier—immortalized their great goalie by establishing the Vezina Trophy, the highest award an NHL goalie can win.

Right: Vezina had just completed his first professional season when featured on this 1911–12 Imperial Tobacco watercolour trading card.

Facing Page: Standing straight and tall in front of his net, Vezina fended off the opposition's finest marksmen with this simple stick and handcrafted goalie skates, circa 1924. A Canadien his entire career, Vezina, a man of quiet dignity, poses here with his 1921-22 teammates.

Harry Watson

"One of the greatest amateur hockey players ever to tear up and down a left wing" is how a 1920s newspaper described Harry "Moose" Watson, who was the star of Canada's Olympic ice hockey championships at Chamonix, France, in 1924.

Born in 1898 in St. John's, Newfoundland, Watson began his hockey schooling at 15 when his family moved to Winnipeg. The following year the Watson family moved to Toronto, and young Harry's St. Andrew's College team made it to the Ontario Hockey Association semifinals only to lose to a Toronto Varsity team that featured the future builder of the Toronto Maple Leafs, Conn Smythe.

After returning from World War I, Watson joined the Toronto Granites. By 1922, The Moose was regularly turning games into routs and commanding the ice with his stickhandling and speed. The Granites dominated Ontario hockey, winning OHA championships in 1920, 1922 and 1923, and the Allan Cup in the latter two seasons. The Toronto Granites played their first Olympic game under the snowcapped peaks of Mont Blanc on January 28, 1924, clobbering Czechoslovakia 30–0. The next day they handed Sweden a 20–0 pasting, and on the third embarrassed the Swiss 33–0. A report sent from that game said it was "a case of going through the motions for the Canadians…" with Watson and Albert McCaffery scoring at will. By the end of the tournament, the Canadians had scored 110 goals and allowed only three to win the gold medal.

When the heroic and resolutely amateur Watson returned to Canada, he was barraged with offers from professional clubs. The owner of the Regina Capitals wooed him with the promise that "most of the boys on our clubs were amateurs until this season, and all are very fine fellows," while the Montreal Maroons took a more direct approach and offered Watson the staggering sum of $30,000. Watson responded by retiring, but came back as player and coach of the 1932 Allan-Cup-winning—and strictly amateur—Toronto Nationals.

Right: *1924 program featuring the Granites, Watson's Canadian champion- ship squad, vs. the Abegweits, the Maritime champions.*

Facing Page: *Harry Watson's personal scrapbook illustrates his outstanding athletic endeavours and is accompanied by his Canada jersey, stick, identity card, dance and dinner card, circa 1924.*

Fashioned over time and influenced by a variety of cultures, the hockey stick has metamorphosed from a well-chosen tree branch to the technical wizardry of featherweight aluminum and finely crafted wood. Pictured left to right: Percy LeSueur's stick with an add-on piece for goaltending, circa 1907; "Cyclone" Taylor's stick with curved shaft and two-piece blade, circa 1908; crudely fashioned barnwood stick with two-piece shaft and blade held together with tin and wire, circa 1890; two sticks from Dan Bain's Winnipeg team, (left) Whitey Merritt's one-piece stick modified with add-on piece for goaltending, and (right) one-piece stick, both circa 1899; one-piece stick with curve in shaft, circa 1880; one-piece stick with circular shaft, circa 1875; one-piece bandy stick, circa 1870; leather gloves with wooden dowelling for protection, circa 1920; long and heavy one-piece stick, circa 1930; early aluminum stick, circa 1940; three-piece stick with steel shaft, wooden ends and replaceable blade, circa 1950; Bill Mosienko's non-fibreglass two-piece hockey stick, circa 1955; Phil Esposito's fibreglass two-piece stick with large curve, circa 1970; aluminum stick with replaceable fibreglass blade, circa 1979; stick with fibreglass shaft (hollowed) and blade, circa 1990; state-of-the-art fibreglass Sherwood stick, circa 1990; fibreglass-wrapped Koho stick, circa 1990; Wayne Gretzky's game pucks from his first four points scored as a Los Angeles King, circa 1988; and Gretzky's 1,000th game, handcrafted silver Easton hockey stick, circa 1993.

CHAPTER FOUR

1926   1942

A New Era

Navy Cut Cigarettes
hockey schedule.
Left: St. Louis Eagles
NHL jersey, circa 1935.

The NHL's first heady steps into a bigger world began in an era known as the Jazz Age, the sparkling, affluent, exuberant recovery that followed the ineffable horrors and deprivations of World War I. American writer Paul Gallico found in his book *The Golden People* a sports epoch brimming with glorious transcendent athletes, who resurrected from the ashes of World War I the possibility that humanity could once more believe in heroes.

"The Golden People," wrote Gallico, were "outstanding not only for their accomplishments, but for the mirror they held up

Syl Apps

Syl Apps first came to the attention of Toronto Maple Leafs boss Conn Smythe in 1934 when one of Smythe's friends saw the athletically versatile Apps play hockey for McMaster University. Smythe was constantly being hounded by touts and he received this report of yet another giant sports talent without enthusiasm, asking merely the player's name. When he heard it was "Sylvanus Apps," Smythe chuckled dismissively. Nobody with the unlikely name of Sylvanus Apps could possibly become a professional hockey player.

Still, Smythe went to watch Apps and was so impressed with his skill at football that he offered him a contract with the Leafs. But Smythe had to wait. Apps, who had won the British Empire pole-vaulting championship in London in 1934, was off to the 1936 Berlin Olympics. He later recalled his London triumph as one of the two most thrilling in his sporting life. The other was leading the Leafs to the 1942 Stanley Cup over Detroit, when Toronto came back from an apparently insurmountable 3–0 deficit to win the next four and take the Cup.

Though a big man, Apps skated with speed and grace, and possessed one of the most accurate shots in the game. He learned to shoot when his father made a small rink by flooding a narrow lane behind the house that led to a garage. Apps nailed a garbage can to its door and fired pucks at the lid, making a racket each time he hit the bull's-eye.

But it was the quieter virtues of skill and finesse that won Apps both the Calder and Byng trophies during his career as a Leaf. He was known for his unselfishness and even tried giving a part of his salary back to a shocked Conn Smythe in 1943 when he missed half a season with a broken leg. The man who once claimed no one named Sylvanus could play hockey said "thanks but no thanks," doubtless wishing generations of Leafs to come would be named Sylvanus.

Right: Apps and his teammates proudly wore their 1941–42 World Championship team jackets.

Facing Page: Leaning against the original Calder Trophy, which Apps won in 1937, is a November 1941 game program illustrating Apps' on-ice determination. This 1941–42 World Champions team photo was taken after Apps captained the Leafs to a come-from-behind Stanley Cup victory. Apps scored his 201st and final goal with this stick, March 21, 1948.

Ace Bailey

"Ace" Bailey's brilliant career with the Toronto Maple Leafs is unfortunately most remembered by how he took leave of it. Bailey, a scoring champ and one of the best penalty killers in the game, was displaying his puck-ragging skills at the Boston Garden on the night of December 12, 1933, with the Leafs two men short. Further down ice, Bruins avenger Eddie Shore was groggily picking himself up from a King Clancy check. Shore, furious, charged the first Leaf he saw—Ace Bailey—who was leaning with his stick on his knees, trying to catch his breath.

Shore ploughed into Bailey's kidneys with his shoulder, catapulting the Maple Leaf into a backward somersault. Players could hear the sickening crack as Bailey's head hit the ice, his skull fractured. As luck would have it, two of the country's most talented brain surgeons were in Boston attending a conference, and over the next three days they performed two intricate, desperate operations on Bailey. Finally, the surgeons surrendered and told waiting reporters and Leafs owner Conn Smythe that they couldn't save Ace—he would be dead within two hours.

As the deathwatch continued outside Bailey's room, the voices of one Nurse Ahn and a colleague could be heard from within. They were trying to revive Ace by slapping him and begging him to get back on the ice, as his team was two men short and needed him badly. Late in the afternoon, a haggard Nurse Ahn emerged to tell all those assembled outside the hospital room that they could go home. Ace Bailey would live.

A benefit game for Ace was held at Maple Leaf Gardens featuring a team of NHL All-Stars against Toronto. Each player skated out to receive his All-Star sweater from Ace Bailey himself, and when Boston's Eddie Shore skated up, Bailey shook hands with the man who had nearly killed him. The building erupted in wild cheering, thus establishing a festive mood of forgiveness and sportsmanship for the NHL's first All-Star game.

Right: Conn Smythe presented Ace with this lifetime gold pass to the Maple Leaf Gardens, circa 1932.

Facing Page: Ace Bailey's last game stick cradles an autographed puck and handcrafted jersey from his 1934 All-Star benefit game. The 1933–34 NHL schedule serves as a grim reminder of how quickly Bailey's presence changed in the game he loved.

King Clancy

"King" Clancy, one of hockey's greatest defencemen and a man whose career would span nearly 70 years, came by his royal title like all kings—through heredity. Clancy's father was a great Ottawa football player in the 1890s, particularly adept at "heeling" the ball out of the scrum and was so nicknamed "King of the Heelers." Clancy junior—appropriate to his abbreviated size—just became "King."

A clever, fearless defender, Clancy put 136 pucks in the net over his 15-year NHL career, all the while keeping up a line of patter that usually managed to deliver him from the hurly-burly unscathed. Once, after goading the Bruins' belligerent Eddie Shore into dropping his gloves, Clancy dropped his, shook Shore's hand and grinned. "Good evening, Eddie, how are you tonight?" Shore convulsed in laughter and Clancy skated away.

Clancy's flamboyant style had not gone unnoticed by Maple Leafs architect Conn Smythe, who thought the best way to counteract the 157-pound defenceman was to buy him from the rival Ottawa Senators. The Senators thought Smythe must be kidding. Clancy was their star player, and besides, there was a great deal of animosity toward him from the Toronto fans. So Senators management asked for $50,000—an extortionate sum for a hockey player in 1930 and one they thought would cool Smythe's ardour.

Smythe didn't have the money, but he loved to gamble. Having just bought a racehorse named Rare Jewel that had never won a race, Smythe wagered all he could on his longshot steed, winning nearly $12,000 when Rare Jewel crossed the finish line first. Smythe borrowed another $20,000 and threw in two players. And so King Clancy became the Leafs' rare jewel: leading them to the Stanley Cup, their first year in Maple Leaf Gardens; making four All-Star teams; becoming head of the NHL referees; and eventually helping to coach the Leafs into the Stanley Cup play-offs in 1972—when the King was 70.

Right: *Gregarious and genial "King" Clancy decorated this CCM poster circa 1931.*

Facing Page: *Noted for running on his skates, a unique form of acceleration, Clancy is depicted on this November 8, 1934, game program breaking away from the opposition, all the while grinning and determined to score. Clancy's "extra special" autographed stick, circa 1925, rests across the Maple Leaf game jersey he wore in his final season in 1937.*

Dit Clapper

Aubrey Victor Clapper, whose childhood attempts to say "Vic" came out "Dit," played 20 seasons with the Boston Bruins, 11 of them as a stalwart on defence. He captained the 1940–41 Bruin team some called the greatest NHL team ever, which included Hall of Famers Frank "Mr. Zero" Brimsek, Milt Schmidt, Woody Dumart and Bill Cowley.

Six-foot-two-inch, 200-pound Clapper was an "athlete's athlete" and used his size to clear space for himself on the ice and finesse one of his 228 goals or 246 assists. As Bruins Hall of Fame goalie Tiny Thompson explained, "Clapper diagnosed the plays like a great infielder in baseball and put himself where he knew the puck had to come."

Clapper, more noted for his peacekeeping than his brawling, is nonetheless responsible for one of the most infamous punches in NHL history. Dit had only one enemy in the league, the fiendish Dave Trottier of the Montreal Maroons. During a 1936 Stanley Cup play-off game, Trottier made the mistake of butt-ending a Bruin rookie. Clapper, enraged, wrestled the miscreant Trottier to the ice and had begun pummelling him when a young referee yanked Clapper up by the hair and impugned the honour of his mother. Clapper, astonished, asked the referee to repeat the slander, and so he did, twice more. Clapper realized he'd been hearing correctly and decked the referee, perhaps the NHL's most cardinal sin.

Clapper, bounced from the game, sat morosely in his hotel lobby fully expecting to be suspended when the battered referee appeared proclaiming, "I want to apologize for saying something to you which caused you to lose your head." The referee then wrote to NHL president Frank Calder: "I was talking when I should have been throwing them into the penalty box." Dit Clapper received only a $100 fine for punching the referee, who turned out to be a future NHL president himself, Clarence Campbell.

Howie Morenz

When Howie Morenz was four years old, he scalded his legs so badly his family thought he'd never walk again, let alone play hockey. Morenz did play hockey, becoming one of the Golden People in the Golden Age of Sport, part of a generation of superb athletes who helped a society recover from World War I and find heroes who wouldn't die. In the 1924–25 season, the Montreal Canadiens star scored 27 goals in 30 games; in 1929–30, he scored 40 goals in 44 games. In all, he scored 270 goals and won the Hart Trophy three times. King Clancy said he was the greatest player he'd ever seen; Billy Boucher called Morenz the "Man O' War" of Hockey.

Yet as Morenz aged, he lost his speed, and the cheers of his beloved fans turned to boos. Heartbroken, Morenz was traded to Chicago, then to New York, destined, it seemed, to become just another journeyman.

Morenz returned to Montreal for the 1936-37 season thanks to his old mentor and Canadiens' coach Cecil Hart. Those who saw Morenz in a Canadiens jersey again the night of January 7, 1937, must have felt Morenz's magic had returned, a half smile playing at the corners of his mouth as he charged up the ice, dominating the game once more. Rushing into the Blackhawk zone, he was knocked off balance and slid into the boards. Chicago's Earl Seibert crashed into him, and the crack of Morenz's leg snapping echoed throughout the rink.

In St. Luke's Hospital, Morenz put on a hearty public front, but privately he worried to linemate Aurèle Joliat that he'd never play again and, pointing to heaven, would watch the Habs "from up there."

Morenz died in his sleep on March 8, 1937, officially from a coronary embolism, but a devastated Aurèle Joliat saw beyond officialdom: "When he realized that he would never play again, he couldn't live with it. I think Howie died of a broken heart."

Right: *Jersey and program from Morenz's 1937 benefit game.*

Facing Page: *Capturing the imagination of an era, Morenz illuminated the game with his stardom. Here he graces the 1927 inaugural issue of* Hockey Magazine, *the* NHL Guide and Record Book, *1932–33, and this* William Patterson *photo trading card, 1924–25. Howie's game stick, circa 1931, and Mappin Trophy, 1927–28 (Canadian Division Leading Scorer) lay alongside his last game jersey of 1937.*

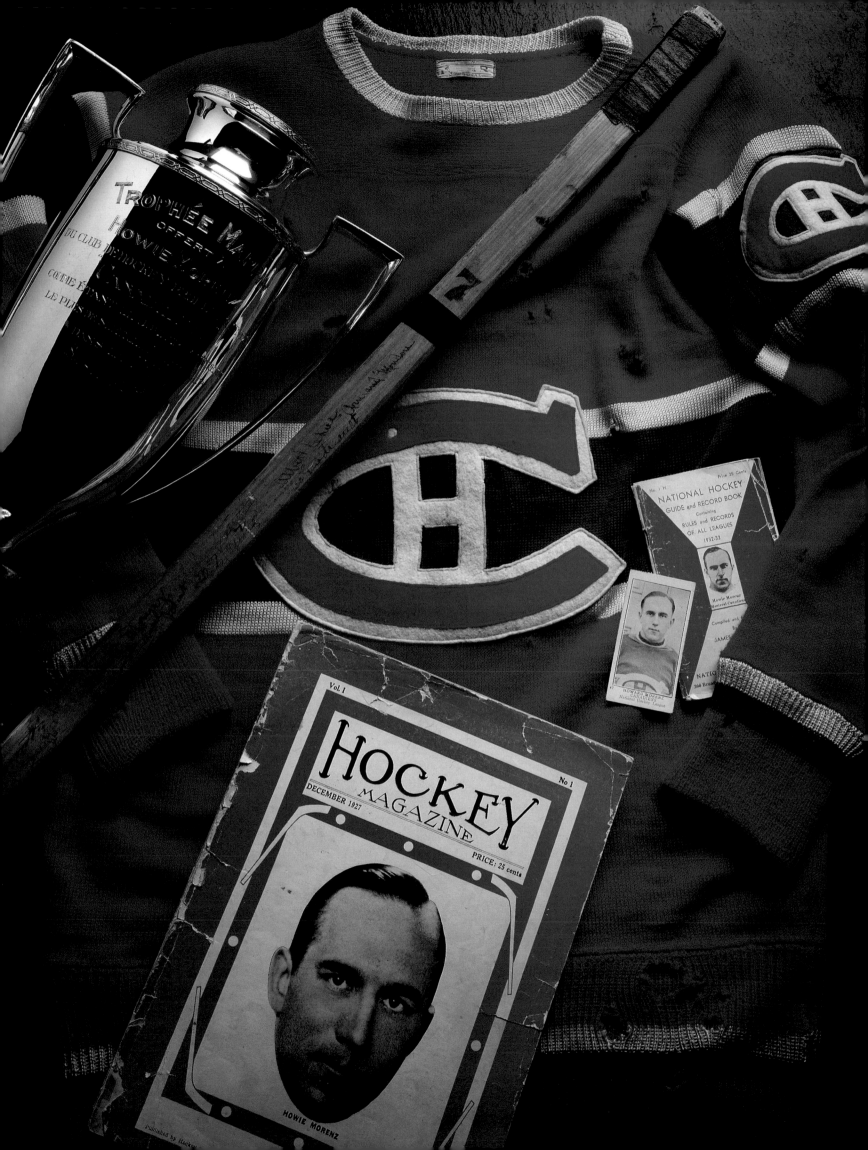

TROPHÉE M...
OFFERT ...
HOWIE ...
DU CLUB DE HOCKEY ...
COMME É...
LE PLU...

NATIONAL HOCKEY
GUIDE and RECORD BOOK
Containing
RULES and RECORDS
OF ALL LEAGUES
1932-33

No. J H   Price 25 Cents

Howie Morenz
Montreal Canadiens

Compiled and ...
JAMES ...
NATIO...
260 Broa...

Vol. I   No. 1

HOCKEY
MAGAZINE
DECEMBER 1927

PRICE: 25 cents

HOWIE MORENZ

Published by Hockey ...

Lester Patrick

A founding member of Hockey's Royal Family, Lester Patrick enjoyed a superlative career that spanned 50 years as player, coach, manager, owner, NHL governor and legend.

Patrick was a swift, graceful skater and a magician with the puck, pioneering defensive innovations while starring with the Montreal Wanderers in 1905–06. After the west coast league he'd established with his brother Frank folded in 1924, Lester went east to become manager of the New York Rangers, whom he would guide to three Stanley Cups.

It was in the second game of the 1928 Stanley Cup final between the Rangers and the Montreal Maroons that Patrick displayed his mettle. Early in the second period, Montreal's Nels Stewart let fly with a bullet that knocked out Rangers' goalie Lorne Chabot. Since teams didn't dress backup goalies, Patrick asked Montreal manager Eddie Gerrard if he could use Ottawa Senators star goalie Alex Connell, who was at the game. Gerrard said no, despite Patrick having let Gerrard use a spare forward against him in a Stanley Cup game a few years earlier. Incensed, the 44-year-old Patrick ripped off his tie and donned the pads himself. A quarter century earlier, Patrick had done the same thing when his Brandon club goalie had to go off for a penalty. He'd stopped the only shot the Ottawa Silver Seven had fired at him.

But that night in 1928, Patrick faced 18 shots from the bloodthirsty Maroons, letting in only one and forcing the game into overtime. Finally, at 7:05 of sudden-death, Billy Boucher won the game for the Rangers, and the crowd of 12,000 gave Patrick a standing ovation. As Cyclone Taylor, another hockey immortal, later said, "There's no one who ever compared with Lester Patrick, the greatest name in hockey history," and it was Patrick's incomparable performance in the nets that spurred his Rangers on to Stanley Cup victory.

Right: The Rangers' Victory song sheet–"Listen to the cheering of the people in the stands; twenty thousand hockey bugs and each a Ranger fan!"

Facing Page: The legend of Lester Patrick is cast in bronze and annually commemorates "outstanding service to hockey in the United States." Another Patrick classic, this photo, circa 1938, depicts Patrick, Ranger trainer Harry Westerby and friend.

Milt Schmidt

Hall of Fame referee Red Storey once boasted: "I'd take five Milt Schmidts, put my grandmother in the net, and we'd beat any team."

The man known as "the fastest playmaker of all time" centred Bobby Bauer and Woody Dumart on the Boston Bruins fabled "Kraut Line." Yet Schmidt, who would win the Art Ross Trophy in 1940 and the Hart Trophy in 1951, came to Boston by accident. In the days before the amateur draft, NHL teams controlled junior teams and prospects within their geographic region. The Kitchener-Waterloo native should have belonged to the Toronto Maple Leafs, but they weren't interested. Bruins Bauer and Dumart pestered Ross to take a look at their talented friend back home until Ross finally agreed, concluding Schmidt was "a nice hockey player, but so terribly small."

In spite of himself, Ross invited Schmidt to training camp, and Schmidt responded with a letter of profound gratitude: "Thank you very much for the invitation. I'm going to work this summer to save enough money to pay my way to training camp." Ross, amused, wrote back that Schmidt needn't work too hard; the Bruins would pay for his ticket.

Schmidt became famous for playing through his injuries and grew up to become the Bruins' six-foot meal ticket, leading Dumart and Bauer to the one-two-three scoring championship in 1940 and two Stanley Cups. Over his 16-year career he scored 229 goals, but the sweetest was his 200th, scored March 18, 1952, when Bobby Bauer came out of retirement to play the night the Bruins honoured Schmidt and Dumart. When Schmidt left hockey to pursue a brilliant coaching career with Boston and later with the Washington Capitals, his former coach Lynn Patrick wished him well: "Milt will have a harder time than I've had. He won't have a guy named Schmidt to throw over the boards when the going gets tough."

Right: Autographed 1952 program from the night Boston honoured greats Milt Schmidt and Woody Dumart.

Facing Page: This black-and-gold Bruins jersey, circa 1937, was worn by Schmidt in his rookie season. He would go on to 16 seasons of glory, banging in his 200th goal with this game stick in 1952. The following year, Parkhurst featured Schmidt's playmaking skills on its 1953 trading card series.

Eddie Shore

It wasn't until he was a student at Manitoba's agricultural college that Eddie Shore took up hockey in response to his older brother's taunts. The more his brother ridiculed him, the harder Shore tried, skating and shooting in 40 below weather.

Ornery, swashbuckling Eddie Shore then spent the next half century cutting a swath through the game, starring with the Boston Bruins to become the first NHL defenceman to win the Hart Trophy four times—and also the first player to regularly wear a helmet after the notorious Ace Bailey incident. The original "Mr. Hockey" later moved upstairs to become the frugal owner-manager of the Springfield Indians, once trading a defenceman for a net.

Shore's feisty determination was spurred on New Year's 1929 when he missed the team train to Montreal, where the Bruins were to play the following night. As there was no air service to Montreal, he borrowed a car and chauffeur from the wealthy Boston friends whose dinner party he was attending and began the long drive. Shore ran straight into a blizzard. The city-born chauffeur wanted to abandon ship, so farm boy Shore drove through the storm with the chauffeur asleep in the back. Exhausted, he traded places with the chauffeur at the border, telling him to go "slow and steady."

Jolted from sleep to find the car in a ditch, Shore hiked to the nearest garage to discover the only tow truck was a hearse. He hitched the hearse to the car, pulled it from the ditch and arrived in Montreal 24 hours after he had set out. A barely coherent Shore made Dit Clapper and Cooney Weiland promise to wake him in an hour, and 60 minutes later they were pouring ice water on their teammate to rouse him. Shore struggled out of bed and into the Forum to score the only goal in a 1–0 Boston victory. Bruins coach Art Ross, unmoved by Shore's superhuman efforts, fined Eddie Shore $200 for missing the train.

Right: *Eddie Shore, who had his nose broken 19 times, decorated this Boston Bruins game program from March 7, 1933.*

Facing Page: *The haunting memory of that fateful night on December 12, 1933, when Shore tragically ended Ace Bailey's career, compelled Shore to don this protective headgear. One of the toughest players in NHL history, Shore's star shone brightly on this O-Pee-Chee 1933–34 trading card.*

Conn Smythe

The man who built the New York Rangers, the Toronto Maple Leafs and Maple Leaf Gardens was one of the most colourful characters ever to grace the hockey world. A much-decorated and wounded veteran of both world wars, whose motto was "If you can't lick 'em in the alley you can't lick 'em on the ice," Conn Smythe always seemed to give one the sense he was guiding his own destiny. Perhaps the fact that his family allowed him to choose his own name when he was seven had something to do with that.

Smythe captained his University of Toronto varsity squad to the 1915 Ontario championships, then coached the U of T Varsity seniors to the 1927 Allan Cup. He caught the eye of the New York Rangers management and agreed to rebuild the Rangers in exchange for $10,000.

The canny Smythe acquired Bill Cook, Frank Boucher, Ching Johnson, and 28 other players for only $32,000. Astonishingly, Rangers president Colonel Hammond listened to Smythe's jealous critics and fired him, shaving $2,500 off Smythe's fee in the process. Rangers owner Tex Rickard heard about the injustice, restored Smythe's original fee and begged him to stay, but it was too late. Smythe returned to Toronto vowing to win the Stanley Cup in revenge. Smythe wagered his $10,000 on a football game and won, then bet his winnings on a Toronto-Ottawa hockey game and won again. Determined to buy the Toronto St. Pats, Smythe together with local worthies bought the team for $164,000, and, always an unblushing patriot, renamed them the Maple Leafs.

In 1931, Smythe, along with J. P. Bickell, used creative financing to build Maple Leaf Gardens—100 yards from where Smythe was born—in an astonishing five months. In 1932, Conn's beloved Maple Leafs won their first of 11 Stanley Cups, thus making good Smythe's promise of revenge and establishing one of the NHL's most illustrious franchises.

Right: Booklet illustrating the building of Maple Leaf Gardens, circa 1956.

Facing Page: Perched upon Madison Square Garden seats, circa 1929, the majestic Conn Smythe Trophy. Assembled artifacts include "Teeder" Kennedy's 1957 jersey, Charlie Conacher's 225th goal stick, autographed stick, circa 1932, and two Gardens' programs, one from the '30s and the other with Smythe on the cover during the war years.

Nels Stewart

Sportswriters of the era used to joke that their friend "Nels" Stewart couldn't skate and couldn't check, but once the puck was on his stick and he could see the whites of the goalie's eyes, then he was as deadly as "Old Poison."

It was a fitting nickname for the big centrepiece of the Montreal Maroons' fabled "S Line." Skating between Hooley Smith and Babe Siebert with short choppy strides, Stewart always seemed to be a day or two behind the play. But when the puck popped in front of the net, the superb reflexes of the all-round athlete would kick in and with the speed of a steel trap snapping shut the puck would leave Old Poison's stick and another goaltender would die a little.

At the time the most heralded rookie to enter the league, Stewart began his career with Montreal in 1925, and with his 34 goals and eight assists in 36 games, led the league in scoring and the Maroons to their first Stanley Cup championship. Stewart picked up the first of his two Hart Trophies for that dazzling debut as the league's most valuable player.

With his rangy six-foot-one-inch, 195-pound frame, Old Poison showed no fear in mowing down those who failed to get out of his way no matter how slowly Stewart might be skating. When he retired in 1940 after tours of duty with the Boston Bruins and New York Americans, Stewart had racked up 953 minutes in penalties—the most of any forward ever in the recorded history of the game.

Nels Stewart also hung up his skates with the greatest scoring record to date. Not only was he the first man to score 300 goals but he finished his brilliant 15-year career with 339 goals and 204 assists for 543 points, regular season and playoffs combined. The record would stand for 13 years, until finally broken by Rocket Richard in 1953.

Right: *New York Americans Nels "Old Poison" Stewart scored his 300th goal with this puck in March 1938.*

Facing Page: *Stewart's skates, circa 1938, propelled him to goal-scoring notoriety throughout his brilliant 15-year career, although his peers often described his skating style as slow-footed.*

NELS STEWART'S
300 TH N.H.L. GOAL
SCORED WITH THIS PUCK
N.Y. AMERICANS VS. N.Y. RANGERS
MARCH 17 TH 1938
PRESENTED TO
FRANK CALDER PRES. N.H.L.

Roy Worters

Roy "Shrimp" Worters was so small a Canadian Customs officer who had come aboard the team train to make a head count couldn't find him. The man approached the New York Americans' star defenceman, the hulking Lionel Conacher, who told the border guard to check Worters's tiny four-by-six-foot sleeping berth. The officer protested that he had already done so, but Conacher told him to check again, since he was sure Worters was "in there somewhere."

Only five feet two inches tall and boasting a playing weight of 130 pounds, the "Phantom Goalie"—so called because of his sorcery between the pipes—was the first goaltender to win the Hart Trophy, which he did in 1928–29 and without much help from his "Vanishing" Americans, who once left Worters to stop 72 shots in a shutout game against Boston.

In 1931, Worters was anointed with the Vezina Trophy and a three-year contract worth an astonishing $8,500 a season. He deserved it: he'd allowed only 74 pucks to get by him, while his plodding teammates put only 76 pucks in opposition nets.

Hall of Fame defenceman Red Dutton recalled how the innovative Shrimp would "use the backs of his hands to divert pucks to the corners, so you very seldom scored on a rebound on Roy. His hands took terrible punishment and I marvel at the little guy and the way he had splints put on his fingers before a game."

Worters breezily dismissed his injuries, saying blood didn't hurt as long as it didn't cloud your vision. Maple Leafs Hall of Famer Charlie Conacher maintained that Worters was the best goalie he'd ever shot pucks at, and ironically it was a blast from Conacher that nailed the little netminder in the windpipe during a game in Worters's hometown, Toronto. The proud goalie finished the game before collapsing into a hospital bed. Worters returned and defied even that stalwart display by braving a severe hernia during the last seven games of his 1936–37—and last—season.

Right: NHL 1932–33 Castrol Sporting Aces schedule. Worters played 45 games that season for the Americans and posted a 2.64 average.

Facing Page: Worters's stars-and-stripes American jersey, circa 1935, is joined by his diminutive game skates of the same period. Tucked neatly inside his skate's leather protector is a Diamond Match Company matchbook from the Silver Hockey Set, 1933–34, showing Worters guarding his crease.

*T*he game on ice passed from one century to another before it saw the creation and acceptance of the goalie mask. From the NHL debut of Clint Benedict's original leather shield in 1930 and Jacques Plante's sculpted fibreglass protector facing NHL shooters in 1959, the mask's development has been influenced by the man behind it— the goaltender. Protection and decoration go hand in hand as evidenced by the following collection of "tribal" facegear. From left to right, bottom row: Jacques Plante's moulded plexi-glass, prototype mask, circa 1956; Jacques Plante's fibreglass mask, debuted in the NHL in 1959; Harold "Boat" Hurley's sculpted plastic mask, circa 1961; another Jacques Plante vented fibreglass mask, circa 1965; Ken Dryden's moulded fibreglass mask, circa 1971. The following masks are all made from handpainted fibreglass, with the exception of those noted. Middle row: Jim Rutherford's mask, circa 1974; Curt Ridley's mask, circa 1975; Clint Benedict's hand-crafted leather protector, circa 1930; Steven Baker's mask, circa 1980; Gilles Gratton's mask, circa 1977. Top row: Ron Low's mask, circa 1978; Wayne Stephenson's mask with adjustable neck protector, circa 1979; Dave Dryden's mask with wire cage, circa 1978; Don Beaupre's mask with wire cage, circa 1982; Ed Belfour's mask with wire cage, circa 1991.

The Original Six

New York Rangers Program, 1959–60 season.
Left: Foster Hewitt's CBC microphone and early broadcast schedule.

The epoch often called "The Golden Era" of hockey began its evolution more like the lead of a medieval alchemist. War in Europe and the Pacific had put such serious physical and financial strains on the game that at times it looked as if the NHL might just be a golden memory.

Early in the 1942–43 season, the NHL had already seen 90 players sign up to fight the Nazi peril—nearly half the puck chasers in the league. The New York (Brooklyn) Americans franchise folded, its lease with Madison Square Gardens about to expire and the team unable to withstand the drain of men and money.

Whitby
Dunlops
1958 world
championship
souvenir
pennant.

Harry Sinden

*The man responsible for guiding
the lavishly celebrated Bobby Orr
from junior hockey into the big leagues
was himself a superior amateur
player, captaining the Whitby Dunlops
to the Canadian senior amateur
championship Allan Cup in 1957,
and to a world amateur victory the
next year. Sinden, as coach and
manager, helped build the Bruin
dynasty that would mature in the
1970s, and came out of coaching
retirement to help guide Team Canada
to their stunning comeback victory
over the Soviets in 1972.*

Some Canadian players were declared "essential" to the Canadian war effort and restricted from crossing the border to play in the U.S. It was even rumoured the American NHL franchises would have to move to Canada since the Canadian government wouldn't give out any more passports, but the rumour turned out to be just another product of wartime paranoia. Overtime periods were cancelled so fans could catch the last train before the blackout. Boston's brilliant "Kraut Line" was rechristened the "Kitchener Kids," and Dudley "Red" Garrett of the New York Rangers became the first player to die in World War II. Then in February 1943, Frank Calder, the man who had presided over the NHL since its birth in 1917, died in office. It was an omen that portended no good.

New York Americans team
crest. Their 16 NHL seasons
came to a close in 1942.

Foster Hewitt's edited hockey broadcasts would console Canadian troops serving in Europe, for as one wrote in a letter to Hewitt: "I was walking past a service hostel right near the Tottenham Court Road tube station when I heard this voice—your voice—coming through the blackout curtains, and I ran in there and it was the hockey broadcast. I damned near cried." Hockey fans continued to champion their game, and Hewitt's voice live from the "Gondola" in Maple Leaf Gardens also comforted fans on the home front, as now more than ever the game offered an escape from a life of rationing and bad news. More important, it offered a realm of heroic action where the heroes didn't die in a mangled, bloody heap. And yet precisely because of the fortunes of war, the league had to adjust to survive: young players who normally would have been in the stands were given a chance to show their mettle under the bright lights, and the teams that did remain afloat consolidated their resources, spawning the dynasties of the "Original Six."

In the 1943–44 season, the NHL Board of Governors decided the game needed an injection of speed, and so began the red line. Until then, forwards had to touch the puck at their own blue line to avoid offsides before continuing up ice. The red line permitted long passes from behind the net to centre, breaking the bonds on fleet forwards and allowing defencemen to be creative.

Speed and elegance became the hallmark of Montreal's "Punch Line" of "Toe" Blake, Elmer Lach and Rocket Richard, and Chicago's "Pony Line," with little men of iron Bill Mosienko and the Bentley Brothers, Doug and Max, imitating Mercury.

Lester Patrick's New York Rangers, though, had been bled dry by men lost to the war, and in 1943–44, Patrick asked permission to temporarily shut down the team. The Montreal Canadiens lent him two of their players, and the beleaguered New Yorkers managed to win a lamentable six games out of 50.

Clarence Campbell, back from the wars, assumed the first of his 31 years as NHL president in 1946, the same year that Gordie Howe suited up for Detroit to begin the first of his epic 34 years in the pros. The following season, the NHL adopted the enlightened social welfare system of the post-war world. Though there had been several benefit games before, the 1947–48 season marked the first annual All-Star game to raise money for the NHL pension fund. Dick Irvin's All-Stars beat Stanley Cup champs the Maple Leafs 4–3.

Rookie Emile "The Cat" Francis brought his prototype trapper's glove when he skated into the nets for the New York Rangers in 1948–a modified

Souvenir puck commemorating Foster Hewitt's Imperial Oil hockey broadcasts, circa 1940.

Bernie Geoffrion

Bernie "Boom-Boom" Geoffrion had a shot like his temperament: blistering and fierce. The feisty right-winger–who many claim perfected if not downright invented the slapshot–won the Calder Trophy in 1952 as the Canadiens' hottest young rival to Rocket Richard. The Art Ross Trophy followed three years later, when the heat from this rivalry had been turned up considerably and had become a very public concern. Richard had a lock on the NHL scoring title when he was suspended near the end of the season for hitting an official. Montreal fans pleaded with Geoffrion to back off on his scoring so Richard would emerge victorious, but Boom-Boom ignored them and beat Richard for the title by one point. Six years later, the same Montreal fans who had booed Geoffrion for eclipsing Richard gave him a 10-minute standing ovation when he became the second NHL player in history–after Rocket Richard–to score 50 goals in a season.

Sportsmen's World Award presented to Geoffrion in 1970.

Alex Delvecchio

Detroit manager Jack Adams had a timeless problem with Time. Sid Abel, the boiler house of the Red Wings' "Production Line" between Gordie Howe and Ted Lindsay, was running out of steam, while the pistons of the Production Line were just heading into their prime. Adams gambled and called up Alex Delvecchio in 1952, when "Fats" was a 20-year-old kid playing left wing on the farm club in Indianapolis.

Delvecchio found himself suddenly in the big time and centring one of the most illustrious lines in the history of hockey. But his superb skating and precision passing combined with his natural aplomb made him the perfect replacement for Sid Abel. Delvecchio would go on to captain the Detroit Red Wings, winning the Lady Byng three times and becoming the second player in NHL history–after Gordie Howe–to play more than 20 seasons for one team.

Delvecchio was in his 14th season with the Red Wings when Parkhurst launched this 1963–64 trading card series.

first baseman's mitt to which he had sewn a leather cuff. Francis had used the glove in junior hockey, and though opposing coach Jack Adams yelled foul, referee King Clancy let Francis use the glove and league president Clarence Campbell swiftly approved it.

The Toronto Maple Leafs ended the decade with a bang, winning three straight Stanley Cups in 1947, '48 and '49, the first NHL team to achieve this milestone. The team featured young Bill Barilko and Howie Meeker, along with future Hall of Famers Turk Broda, Ted Kennedy and Syl Apps. Maple Leaf Gardens pioneered the conveniences contemporary hockey fans take for granted, installing protective glass in 1948, escalators in 1955 and separate penalty boxes in 1963.

The Detroit Red Wings locked up the Prince of Wales Trophy and hid the key. They took the league championship eight times from 1942 to 1955 and the Stanley Cup five times. The "Production Line" of Gordie Howe, Ted Lindsay and Sid Abel burned up the 1950s scoring charts, and Terry Sawchuk, crouched and scowling before the Red Wing nets, dared any puck to cross the line.

The Hart Memorial Trophy honours the NHL's most valuable player.

Live televised hockey broadcasts began in Canada in the autumn of 1952, with the first *Hockey Night in Canada* from Maple Leaf Gardens beaming out on November 1. The Chicago Blackhawks experimented with weekend afternoon games since general manager Bill Tobin didn't think the Hawks could compete with Saturday night television. He was right, and Chicago Stadium attendance rose by 5,000.

The Montreal Canadiens were elevated to a class unto themselves by the genius of Rocket Richard, who netted his 500th NHL goal in 1958.

They eclipsed the Maple Leafs' record of four straight Stanley Cups by winning five in a row beginning in 1956, a record that still stands. The Habs, in fact, nearly won eight. They took home the Cup in 1953 but lost it in Game Seven for the next two years. The players' roster reads like a pantheon of the Hockey Hall of Fame: Jacques Plante, Maurice and Henri Richard, Jean Béliveau, Boom-Boom Geoffrion, Dickie Moore, Doug Harvey and Tom Johnson all wore the bleu, blanc et rouge.

In 1957, the Blackhawks signed Bobby Hull, who bulldozed them to the Stanley Cup in 1961, tied Rocket Richard's 50-goals-in-a-season record in 1962 and then broke it in 1966 by blasting 54 pucks into opposition nets.

In 1962–63, the introduction of the amateur draft broke the stranglehold some NHL teams held on promising new talent. Until then, major league clubs had sponsored junior teams and "protected" their best players when it came time for them to turn pro. The change helped teams such as New York and Boston, who had spent much of the past two decades on the low end of the standings. By 1966, sponsorship of junior teams had ended, though the Boston Bruins managed to salvage an ace. Bobby Orr, who had augured great things for the Bruins ever since he was a 14-year-old junior with Oshawa, donned the black and gold of Boston. The team's fortunes were to change dramatically over the next decade with the rise of Bobby Orr, and in 1967, there was an expanding of the collective rink with the addition of six new teams. The Golden Era of the Original Six came to a close—the age of expansion had begun.

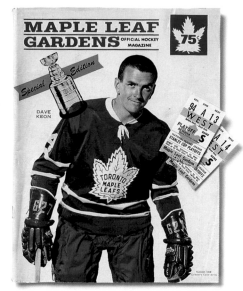

Maple Leafs program and ticket stubs from the 1967 Stanley Cup play-offs.

Introductory booklet for the novice fan, circa 1951.

Dave Keon

An alumnus of Toronto's renowned St. Michael's College, Davey Keon was a fast skater and ace stickhandler who scored 20 goals in the first of his 15 seasons with the Leafs and won the Calder Trophy as the league's top rookie. Keon's combination of excellence and fair play earned him the Lady Byng Trophy twice. His deft goal-scoring touch in the play-offs gave the Leafs 22 goals in four Stanley Cup victories– three of them in succession–and won Keon the Conn Smythe Trophy as the most valuable player in the Leafs' 1967 Stanley Cup championship.

The Stanley Cup has expanded throughout the years to feature the names of the victorious–these uneven bands are circa 1940.

Tim Horton

One of the strongest men in hockey, Tim Horton combined power with brains to become a great rushing and playmaking defenceman.

Six-time All-Star Horton shored up the Leafs defence and played on four Stanley Cup winners. In 1965, when the Leafs were in a slump, coach "Punch" Imlach moved Horton up to right wing alongside "Red" Kelly and George Armstrong. Horton, with his raging slapshot, scored 12 goals. The amiable Horton often ran afoul of Imlach, and once, after the player had started his chain of doughnut shops and was getting grief about "doughnuts vs. hockey," Horton brought a carton of stale ones to practice and used them as pucks. Tim Horton played his last game in Maple Leaf Gardens, but this time as

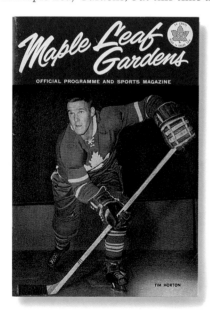

Maple Leaf Gardens 1963
Stanley Cup game program.

a Buffalo Sabre. He was killed in a car accident while driving home from that game on February 21, 1974. He was 44.

Referee Red Storey wore this jersey as a linesman in the mid-1960s.

Roy Storey

Dauntless "Red" Storey, an NHL referee from 1951 to 1959, officiated more than 2,000 hockey games from amateur to pro, earning a reputation for bravery under fire. A superb athlete himself, Storey once scored a still unbroken record of 12 goals in a lacrosse game in Quebec, and ran for three touchdowns in the fourth quarter to give the Toronto Argonauts a 30–7 victory over Winnipeg and the 1938 Grey Cup. Storey was still revelling in that victory when his phone rang, and Lloyd Blinco, general manager of the AHL's Hershey Bears, told him they were expecting trouble at that night's play-off game in New Haven. They needed a stouthearted man like Red to come down and keep the peace, and besides, there was a private plane to fly him down in style. When Storey arrived at the airport, he was met by a match-chewing character who turned out to be his pilot. The "private plane" turned out to be a tiny box of aluminum, and when Storey's door wouldn't shut, the pilot told him not to worry, the air pressure would hold him in. The flight

was a nightmare; the pilot confessed he'd never flown in the dark or to this particular airport. Storey believed him when they nearly landed on the bright lights of an oil refinery. When a shaken Storey finally arrived midway through the first period, the game had turned into a melee. Storey, now extremely foul of mood, donned the stripes and put the game–and the cosmos–back in order: "The first guy that glanced at me got a penalty and suddenly everybody became little gentlemen. There was no more trouble."

•

Jean Ratelle

Jean Ratelle's sublime hockey intelligence and playmaking skills, combined with his deep sense of honour and dignity, once moved a teammate to say, "He functions on a different level from the rest of us. He's the kind of man we'd all like to be." Ratelle spent 13 of his 20 NHL seasons in New York, where he centred Rod Gilbert and Vic Hadfield on the Rangers' flashy and prolific "G.A.G.(Goal A Game) Line." Ratelle won the Lady Byng Trophy twice, the Lester Pearson Award as the NHL's most valuable player as voted by his peers, and the Bill Masterton Trophy for his dedication to hockey and elevation of the game. But he still remained a touch wistful about his hockey accomplishments. "I'd trade almost everything for one Stanley Cup," he told one sportswriter. Ratelle never sipped champagne from the "Jug," but when he retired in 1981 as the league's sixth highest

Jean Ratelle's 250th NHL goal stick, circa 1973.

point scorer, he left a legacy of sportsmanship that embodied all of the virtues symbolized by the Stanley Cup.

Doug Harvey

Doug Harvey was one of the most talented defencemen ever to play in the NHL, winning the Norris Trophy seven times as the league's premier defender, and marshalling the likes of Rocket Richard, Jean Beliveau and Dickie Moore to six Stanley Cups– five of them in succession. Possessed of legendary control, Harvey would use his marvellous skills to speed up or slow down a game, frustrating his opponents and helping to create the seemingly unstoppable Montreal Canadiens dynasty of the 1950s.

Montreal Forum souvenir program, 1960–61.

Red Kelly

Leonard Patrick "Red" Kelly graduated from Toronto's St. Michael's College, renowned for producing hockey stars, and went straight to the Detroit Red Wings in 1947. There he starred on defence for 12 seasons, becoming the first winner of the James Norris Memorial Trophy as the NHL's top defenceman, and a four-time winner of the Lady Byng Trophy. An extremely clean defender who could check in the corners without boarding

Parkhurst's 99-card set featured "Red" Kelly in 1963-64.

or cross-checking, Kelly could also lead the rush, which Toronto Maple Leaf coach Punch Imlach counted on when he traded for Kelly in 1960 and made him a centre. Kelly played seven seasons with the Leafs and, after retiring in 1967, coached the unremarkable Los Angeles Kings expansion team into the play-offs for the next two seasons. Kelly played in a record-setting 19 Stanley Cup play-off series, winning Lord Stanley's trophy eight times.

Bill Barilko

"The Hero of Leaf Cup Win" shouted the Toronto Globe & Mail headlines about young Toronto defenceman Bill Barilko, and so he was. On April 21, 1951, the Maple Leafs were down two goals to one to the Montreal Canadiens with less than a minute to play in Game Five of the Stanley Cup finals. When Toronto's Tod Sloan scored with only 32 seconds left in regulation time, everyone in Maple Leaf Gardens realized this would make the fifth game of five to be decided in overtime in the nail-biting series. At 2:53 of sudden death, with the Leafs pressing in the Montreal zone, Barilko stretched to keep Howie Meeker's pass from sliding over the blue line. Off balance and about to go airborne, Barilko fired the puck high into the Montreal net to give the Leafs the win and the Stanley Cup. The crowd of 14,477 went wild, and Barilko's jubilant mother ran onto the ice to kiss her heroic son, while Canadiens manager Frank Selke, whose team had suffered from Barilko's devastating body checks, muttered, "I hate that Barilko so much I sure wish we had him with the Canadiens." Sadly, the world would not have Bill Barilko much longer. Four months later, the Globe & Mail announced that the Hero, who had gone to Northern Ontario on a post-season fishing trip, had been killed in a plane crash. He was 24.

Barilko's 1951 Stanley–Cup–winning skate and puck.

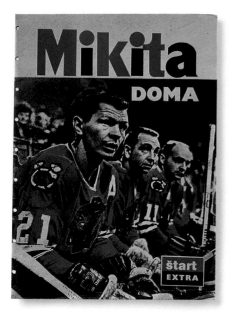

This Czechoslovakian magazine, circa 1967, devoted its entire issue to native son Stan Mikita.

Stan Mikita

Stan Mikita, the Chicago Blackhawks' ace centreman, has a compendium of firsts to his credit: the first Czechoslovakian-born player in the NHL; the first man to win the Art Ross, Hart and Lady Byng trophies all in the same year (which he did twice); and, according to Bobby Hull, the man who invented the curved stick, an innovation that made the puck slide and dip like a fastball. Mikita had become angry during a practice and tried to break his stick by jamming it between the boards and the hinges of the players' bench gate. But the stick wouldn't snap. When he pulled it out, the blade had curved dramatically, and Mikita started shooting pucks at the net. As Hull recalled, "I thought he had gone goofy but he skated up to me and said, 'Gee Bobby, I tried to break my stick and put a hook in it. Can you ever shoot the puck!'" As Mikita would repeatedly prove, racking up 1,394 points in 22 seasons.

Clarence Campbell

Clarence Campbell always answered his telephone at NHL headquarters in Montreal with his trademark

Mikita's curved stick.

"Campbell, here," and for 31 years he was there, discharging his duties as NHL president with a civilized mien befitting a former Rhodes scholar. Yet Campbell was no aloof elitist but rather a populist who often found himself fielding questions as he worked late into the night: "I suppose I've settled more beer-hall arguments and bets about hockey than any man alive."

Campbell returned to Canada after serving in World War II, having won the Order of the British Empire for his work as a prosecutor with the Canadian War Crimes Commission in Germany. Scrambling for a job like other returning vets, the former NHL referee wrote to the NHL head office asking for any work they could give him.

President Red Dutton summoned Campbell to Montreal for an interview. "We were walking across Dominion Square in Montreal when Dutton told me he was going to resign and recommend me as president. At noon that day I had the job [$10,000 a year] and two years income so I'd have time to rehabilitate myself if they fired me."

So Clarence Campbell, who had at best hoped for some junior position,

The Clarence Campbell Bowl is presented to the winner of that conference.

suddenly found himself president of the League, and through his dedicated stewardship and firm resolve the NHL grew and prospered from a six-team organization to one boasting 18 teams by the time Campbell retired in 1977.

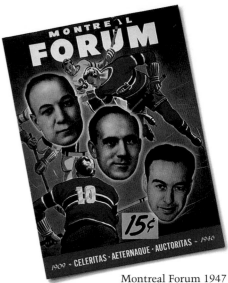

Montreal Forum 1947 commemorative program featuring Toe Blake alongside Morenz and Lalonde.

Toe Blake

Hector "Toe" Blake won the NHL's prestigious Hart and Art Ross trophies in 1938-39 as the league's leading scorer and most valuable player, and in his 14 seasons with Montreal would star on the Canadiens' walloping "Punch Line" with Elmer Lach and Rocket Richard, win two Stanley Cups and the Lady Byng Trophy. Toe returned to coach the Canadiens in 1955-56, his competitive spirit aflame as he stood in the dressing room exhorting a new generation of Habs to show "speed and strength." To remind them that his interest in their continuing excellence was more than professional, Blake would point to the words of Canadian poet John McRae, which were inscribed on the Habs dressing room wall in red block letters: "To you with failing hands we throw the torch/Be yours to hold it high..." Blake's players took up the torch, winning their coach eight more Stanley Cups before his retirement in 1968.

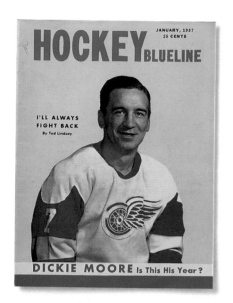

I'LL ALWAYS FIGHT BACK
By Ted Lindsay

DICKIE MOORE Is This His Year?

Lindsay's finest season found him on the January 1957 cover of *Hockey Blueline*.

Ted Lindsay

"Terrible" Ted Lindsay, a swaggering, fearless left-winger, won the Art Ross Trophy in 1950 as the NHL's leading scorer. He generated 78 points in 69 games playing alongside Sid Abel and Gordie Howe on Detroit's incomparable Production Line, the Red Wings' physical and emotional heart from 1948 to 1955, when the mighty Wings won the Stanley Cup four times. Lindsay was a master of defence, sometimes playing the two-way game with a bit too much enthusiasm, which earned him nearly 2,000 minutes in penalties and several fines in his 17 seasons with the pros. Ironically, Lindsay's intelligent leadership qualities led to his trade, when Detroit manager Jack Adams found Terrible Ted's groundbreaking role as NHL Players' Association president to be disruptive and sent him to Chicago in 1957. Lindsay played three years with Chicago, retired, then came back to

Detroit for one final championship season in 1964–65, retiring as the highest scoring left-winger in NHL history to that date.

———•———

The Norris and Wirtz Families

The Norrises of Detroit and the Wirtzes of Chicago make up one of professional hockey's most legendary dynasties. Both families have been involved in NHL team ownership since 1933 when Arthur M. Wirtz and the father-and-son team of James and James D. Norris bought the financially troubled Detroit Olympia arena and the Detroit Falcons. The prudent purchase would relaunch the team into orbit as the Red Wings and one of the NHL's great franchises.

In 1935, the trio bought Chicago

Chicago Blackhawks jersey, circa 1935.

Stadium, and 19 years later, James Norris, Jr., and Arthur Wirtz took control of the faltering Blackhawks, which they rebuilt into another of the NHL's prestige franchises, and which Wirtz's son Bill still owns and operates.

With the death of James Norris, Sr., in 1952, his 25-year-old daughter Marguerite

took over the Red Wings. She became the first female president–and youngest boss–in the NHL, a position she astutely held for 18 months and one Stanley Cup before handing the team over to her brother Bruce, who stayed on at the helm until poor health moved him to sell the family business in 1982.

———•———

Bill Gadsby

"The Great Gadsby" endured a series of brutal hardships that seemed to come from the pages of fiction but were real enough to the Calgary-born defensive virtuoso for Chicago, New York and Detroit. While returning from England with his mother at the beginning of World War II, the 12-year-old Gadsby's ship was torpedoed, and he spent five hours in the freezing Atlantic before being plucked to safety. In 1952, while in his playing prime as captain of the Blackhawks, Gadsby was crippled with polio and told he would never play again. Yet if the boy could not be sunk by torpedoes, the big, left-handed defenceman swore he would not be scuppered by polio. He fought back and won, playing for the Hawks until 1954, then lending his considerable defending talents to the Rangers for six years and the Red Wings for five. Gadsby made seven All-Star appearances in his 20-year NHL career. •

The Coca-Cola company featured NHL stars on their bottle caps in the mid-1960s.

Jack Adams

In late November 1919, a plaintive, urgent telegram came down the CPR line from Vancouver to Jack Adams in Toronto: "Our team in very bad shape. Skinner has twisted knee cartilage and Duncan with shoulder ligaments both out of game for month or more. I would greatly appreciate if you would make a big effort to come and help us out. Situation desperate or would not wire you. Frank A. Patrick."

It was hard to ignore a royal summons, so Adams packed up and headed west, where in 1922 he won the PCHA scoring title with 25 goals in 24 games, and six more in the Stanley Cup series that Vancouver lost to Toronto.

It is easy to forget that Jack Adams was an uncommonly fine player, such is the vast scope of the contribution from the man who was "Mr. Detroit Red Wings" for 35 years. Adams joined the Detroit Falcons in 1927, the city's first year in the NHL. As the shaky team needed a coach for the second season, Jack Adams went to league president Frank Calder and asked for the job. Calder gave it to him and wished him well, never imagining he had just sanctioned the continuation of a hockey legend.

The early years were fraught with the difficulties faced by any new franchise and compounded by the misery of the Great Depression. In 1933, James Norris, Sr., the Canadian-born, American-based grain and shipping tycoon, bought the renamed Red Wings and called Adams into his office to tell him, "You can have this job on probation for one year to see how you make out."

Adams made out rather well. Under his hearty, dynamic tutelage, the Red Wings won back-to-back Stanley Cups in 1936 and 1937, 12 league championships and five more Stanley Cups over the next 35 years. Jack Adams, who was also passionately involved in junior hockey and community charities, became the first winner of the Lester Patrick Trophy for service to hockey in America.

Right: *Silver anniversary tray presented to Adams by the "Original Six" teams.*

Facing Page: *Adams's miniature Stanley Cup, presented by the NHL for 50 years of "outstanding service to the game," sits on a Detroit Olympia arena chair, circa 1930. Souvenir puck, telegrams from fans, circa 1940–50, Adams Toronto Arenas portrait, circa 1918, and Gordie Howe's jersey, circa 1965, share the spotlight.*

George Armstrong

George Armstrong never considered himself much more than an average hockey player, claiming his skating was ordinary and his shot wouldn't break glass. Yet Toronto Maple Leaf coach Hap Day rated his big forward among the top guns in the league: "I've seen Armstrong skate the length of the ice to make his play and score a goal and there aren't many players who can do that."

George Armstrong was known and loved as "The Chief," partly because of his mother's Iroquois heritage, partly because Alberta's Stoney Indian tribe christened him "Big-Chief-Shoot-the-Puck" when Armstrong's Allan-Cup-winning senior team made a western tour. "Army" captained the Leafs for 12 of his 21 seasons, and, as Conn Smythe personally appointed his captains, Armstrong was the ninth and last elevated by Smythe, who said "the Chief is the best captain, as a captain, that the Leafs have ever had."

Armstrong's perseverance and leadership were spawned by childhood adversity. A bout of spinal meningitis, which his father said later affected his skating and made him work harder, laid him low at age six. His mother saw it differently, once saying George "suffered a lot as a boy because he was an Indian. He told me the reason he battled so hard all these years is because of those days."

Yet when Armstrong felt his legs were going, he retired after the 1967–68 season. The Leafs weren't the same without him, nor The Chief without them. One sleepless night after a 3–1 loss to the Rangers, Punch Imlach's phone rang in his New York hotel suite. On the other end was George Armstrong, who humbly asked, "Do you think I could help the club if I came out of retirement?" The answer was yes, and Armstrong, who had been a money player in the Leafs' four Stanley Cup victories, came back to help them into the play-offs one more time.

Right: This novelty record, "Maple Leafs Hockey Talks," featured interviews with 1960s Leaf stars.

Facing Page: Decorated with ceremonial eagle feathers, Armstrong's 275th goal stick, circa 1969, stands tall beside his 1966 Leaf jersey. Armstrong recorded his second highest point total in 1966, tying his 1960 production of 51 points and only two shy of his best-ever 1962 Stanley-Cup-year total of 53.

Johnny Bower

Johnny Bower was always on the wrong side of the age game. After sneaking into the Canadian army as an underaged 16-year-old in 1940, Bower was still young enough to play junior when he was discharged, causing teams to dispute that anyone who had spent four years at the wars was certainly too old for junior hockey. Since no one could find Bower's birth certificate however, he played out the season and turned pro with Cleveland of the AHL in 1945 at 21.

It wasn't until Bower was 34 that he made it to the NHL for keeps, when the Maple Leafs drafted him in 1958. When Bower arrived at the border on his way to Toronto, a U.S. immigration officer scoffed at his claim to be a goalie, saying he was "too old."

Bower, whose family had suffered during the Depression, was reluctant to give up his security in the minors when drafted by the Leafs. Even after 70 games for the New York Rangers in 1953–54 and five more in 1955, Bower was sent back to the minors, teaching him how fragile an NHL career could be. "I kept telling Toronto I couldn't help them, but they warned me if I didn't sign they would suspend me."

Bower, with characteristic modesty, had underestimated his value to the Leafs. The poor boy who played goal because his family couldn't afford skates backstopped Toronto to four Stanley Cups and won the Vezina Trophy twice: once alone and once with Terry Sawchuk.

In his 11 full seasons with the Leafs, Bower won the J. P. Bickell Award three times as the team's most valuable player, inspiring the team with his formidable work ethic. "John gave everything he had in workouts," said Leaf captain George Armstrong, "and we weren't going to let an old guy show us up." Detroit's manager Jack Adams also noticed that the aging Bower was adept at showing up the Red Wings: "The big guy [Frank Mahovlich] keeps putting them in, and the old guy keeps kicking them out."

Right: *After 17 maskless NHL seasons, Bower adopted this face protector in 1969–70.*

Facing Page: *In 1967, 43-year-old Bower patrolled the Maple Leaf goal line wearing these skates and pads. Bower finished the season with a 2.63 goals-against average and helped bring home the Stanley Cup to Toronto for the fourth time in six seasons.*

Turk Broda

When Tom Gaston, a young Toronto Maple Leafs fan who had been blinded in an industrial accident, had his bandages removed, he found vision had returned to one of his eyes. Still, Tom wondered if his newly restored sight was playing tricks on him. There was another man in the room besides his father—a man who looked like Toronto Maple Leafs beloved goalie, "Turk" Broda. And it was Broda, who knew young Gaston from seeing him around Maple Leaf Gardens and now wanted to be one of the first people Gaston would—if he could—see.

The charitable and lovable Broda would become one of hockey's greatest money goalies of all time but still kept the game in a healthy perspective. "The Leafs pay me for my work in the practices," joked Turk, "and I throw in 60 NHL games for nothing."

Broda's arduous work in practices was legendary, especially so at Christmas 1949, when Conn Smythe put the pudgy Broda on a very public diet: "I'm taking him out of the nets and he's not going back until he shows some common sense." Broda lived on fruit juice, and coach Hap Day put the "Crisco Kid" in a shooting gallery during practice, relieving Broda of his stick and getting three or four players to fire pucks at him simultaneously. Broda sweated off the extra seven pounds and returned to a grateful team.

Turk, who earned his nickname as a child when his neck would turn turkey red if he got angry, spent 16 years between the pipes for the Toronto Maple Leafs, twice winning the Vezina Trophy, establishing a Stanley Cup record of 13 shutouts in 101 play-off games, and backstopping the Leafs to five Stanley Cup victories. In the 1950–51 Stanley Cup final, Rocket Richard credited Toronto's upset victory to one man—Turk Broda: "I couldn't beat him. Toe Blake couldn't. None of the Canadiens could."

Right:
Leaf goaltenders Al Rollins and "Turk" Broda grin and bear the public scrutiny of their respective playing weights, Sporting World, *circa 1951.*

Facing Page:
Outfitted in this classic Leaf jersey, circa 1942, and goalie stick, circa 1940, Broda backstopped the Leafs to their surprising 1942 Stanley Cup victory. Broda smiles back at us from the November 2, 1946, Maple Leaf Gardens program.

MAPLE LEAF
GARDENS
MAPLE LEAF GARDEN
LEAF GARDENS
OFFICIAL PROGRAMME
15¢
TORONTO
MAPLE
LEAFS

John Bucyk

Johnny Bucyk, the concrete block of a left-winger from Edmonton, played on two of the most celebrated Boston lines in Bruin history, first with Bronco Horvath and Vic Stasiuk on the "Uke Line," and later with Ken Hodge and Phil Esposito during Boston's triumphal return to the top of the league and two Stanley Cup victories in the 1970s.

"The Chief," so named because a Boston cartoonist thought Bucyk's face more representative of Alberta's Blackfoot tribe than of his ancestral Ukraine, suffered through eight pathetic seasons with Boston in which they did not once qualify for the play-offs. Yet the Chief transcended the mediocrity, averaging more than 20 goals a year and finishing among the top 10 NHL point scorers.

In the first half of the 1967–68 season, Bucyk generated a Bruin run that took the team from last place to first, and with his devastatingly accurate shot scored 29 goals and 39 assists.

Known as "Digger" by his teammates because he could mine the puck out of a crowd, and as "Lurch" by opposing goaltenders because of his hulking and unmovable presence near the goalposts, Bucyk twice managed to win the Lady Byng Trophy for sportsmanlike play while maintaining a deserved reputation for toughness. "Lady Byng or not," Bobby Orr said, "I never knew anyone who could hit harder, especially with the hip check."

Bucyk modestly attributed his endurance to the circumstances of his impecunious boyhood in Edmonton, where he would always carry his skates and stick with him to maximize the free ice time opportunities he'd get for sweeping the ice and stands at the local rink. Bruin coach Harry Sinden saw in Bucyk something more than a hardworking Ukrainian kid, saying in 1974, "You need six great players—one in each position—to get anywhere in professional hockey. Next to Bobby Hull I would rate John Bucyk as the greatest left-winger in the last 15 years."

Right: Miniature Prince of Wales Trophy awarded to each of the Boston Bruins as NHL champions for 1973–74.

Facing Page: Boston Garden seats from the 1970s reserve a place for Bucyk's final-season 1978 jersey, his 51st career high goal stick, April 3, 1971, (left) and his 350th NHL career goal stick, February 23, 1971, (right).

Bill Durnan

"Big Bill" Durnan entered the NHL elite when he was 28 years old—an age when other players are planning their retirement. Before that, Durnan had starred in the minors, earning decent money without the stresses of a big league goalie.

But Durnan's talent was big league, and for three seasons Montreal Canadiens manager Tommy Gorman watched him and waited. Gorman, known for signing players at terms favourable to the Habs, finally struck in 1943. But he had met his match. The first game of the season was about to start and Durnan still hadn't signed his contract. Gorman, sweating, gave in and offered Durnan the contract he wanted. Durnan signed it, and Gorman had the satisfaction of telling him to suit up. A startled Durnan pulled on his gear and held the Bruins to a 2–2 draw. In his stunning first season with the Canadiens, Durnan allowed only 109 goals in 50 games, and 14 more in nine play-off games, winning him the Vezina Trophy. Durnan would soon own the Vezina, becoming the first goalie to win it four years straight and the first to win it six times.

Durnan was the first ambidextrous goalie, wearing a combination of catching mitt and stick glove on both hands that allowed him full advantage of his expert catching reflexes honed during his years of off-season baseball.

During the 1948–49 campaign the easygoing Durnan set a modern shutout record, blanking the opposition until Chicago Blackhawk Gaye Stewart scored on March 9, 1949, to end Durnan's 309 minute and 20 second streak.

Though Big Bill had repeatedly advocated NHL clubs carry a backup goalie to lessen the strain on the starter, his requests went unheeded. And so, in 1950, only seven years after he began his NHL career, and claiming his "nerves were shot," the man often called the greatest goaltender of modern times retired.

Right: Five years after retirement, Durnan was featured in the 1955–56 Parkhurst "Old Time Great" trading card series.

Facing Page: Durnan's ambidextrous catching gloves, circa 1949, played an important role in his brilliant career. The ability to use either hand to catch pucks or wield this goalie stick, circa 1945, was a skill Durnan had learned as a youngster playing in a Toronto church league.

Glenn Hall

Glenn Hall wasn't always in that much of a hurry to block rocketing bits of frozen rubber with his body, and sometimes showed up late for training camp because he hadn't finished painting his barn. One of hockey's most original characters, the 11-time All-Star goaltender played 18 seasons in the NHL, 10 with Chicago bookended by four each with Detroit and St. Louis. Though winner of the Calder Trophy, the Conn Smythe Trophy, the Stanley Cup and the Vezina three times, Hall had a rocky relationship with the game. Before each match he would get down on his hands and knees and throw up.

"There's nothing really wrong with my stomach," Hall once explained. "But on the day of a game, or on a day when I face something I don't particularly want to do, nothing helps."

Yet the emotional Hall was ruthlessly cool in the nets, leading the NHL in shutouts for six seasons, playing in 115 Stanley Cup play-off games, and setting an NHL record for most consecutive games by a goalie. The 502-game odyssey stretched from 1955 to November 7, 1962, when Hall leaned down to adjust a toestrap on his pad and upon trying to straighten up found that his back refused to cooperate.

Hall had been notoriously protective of his job ever since the precocious 10-year-old elected himself to play net for his school team in the hockey country of Humboldt, Saskatchewan, a place that claims to have 10 months of winter and two months of tough sledding. "I was the captain of the hockey club, the coach and manager and everything else. I had to ice the team. Nobody else would go into the net so I played goalie and rather enjoyed it."

Hall, who often claimed he'd been meaning to retire since age 15, did so at 40 after leading the expansion St. Louis Blues into three Stanley Cup finals.

Right: Souvenir program features Hall in his seventh 70-game season of uninterrupted play.

Facing Page: Ending a 22-year Stanley Cup drought, Hall, in this finely stitched Chicago jersey, delivered the Stanley Cup to Chicago fans in 1961. Hall posted an impressive regular season goals-against average of 2.57 and an even better 2.25 average in the play-offs.

CHICAGO·STADIUM REVIEW hockey program 25¢

1961-62 SEASON...

BLACK HAWKS

Gordie Howe

One freezing winter's day during the Depression, a poor woman came to the door of Gordie Howe's childhood home in Floral, Saskatchewan. She was peddling a threadbare sack of odds and ends to buy milk for her children, and Howe's mother took pity on her, scraping together two dollars. When six-year-old Howe and his mother emptied the sack, out tumbled a pair of skates. He and sister Edna trundled off to the frozen potato patch, Edna taking one skate, Howe the other. But one-legged skating proved unsatisfactory and as Howe later recalled, "It wasn't long before I had both skates."

The boy with one skate went on to rewrite hockey's record books during his 34 year career, winning four Hart Trophies and leading the Detroit Red Wings to as many Stanley Cups. His first NHL goal came against Leafs goalie Turk Broda on October 16, 1946. Eighteen years later, Howe netted goal 627 to become the league's all-time scoring leader and holder of practically every NHL record: most games played; most goals, assists and points in both regular season and play-offs.

When Howe hung up his skates after 25 years with the Wings, he said: "Say I retired, not quit. I don't like the word quit." And indeed, he didn't. He played for the Houston Aeros and the New England Whalers in the World Hockey Association and again in the NHL with Hartford, passing more bittersweet milestones: the first player over 50 to score an NHL goal; the first to play on the same line as his sons.

"The best fun I know is skating in an empty rink after practice," Howe once said. "I like the 'whunk' sound the puck makes when I drive it against the boards." And so the man who began his career on one skate, and was known worldwide as "Mr. Hockey," still had his heart in that frozen potato patch of childhood.

Right: Detroit-Montreal game tickets for November 10, 1963, the night Howe scored his 545th goal and eclipsed Rocket Richard's NHL record.

Facing Page: "Mr. Hockey's" Detroit away jersey, circa 1966, game-weathered gloves, circa 1952–53 (note inscription) and 600th NHL career goal stick from November 27, 1965, surround the quintessential trading card: Parkhurst's 1963–64 series, number 55 of a 99-card set.

Frank Mahovlich

In 1961, 23-year-old Frank Mahovlich potted a dazzling 48 goals and looked to be as incendiary a hockey force as Rocket Richard. Two years later, in a suite at Toronto's Royal York Hotel, Detroit Red Wings owner James Norris offered Maple Leafs owner Harold Ballard the breathtaking sum of $1 million for the man they called "The Big M." Ballard agreed in principle, and Norris forked over 10 crisp $100 bills as a down payment. Yet when dawn broke, Ballard realized that a million bucks for Frank Mahovlich probably wouldn't be a fair trade. At least not yet.

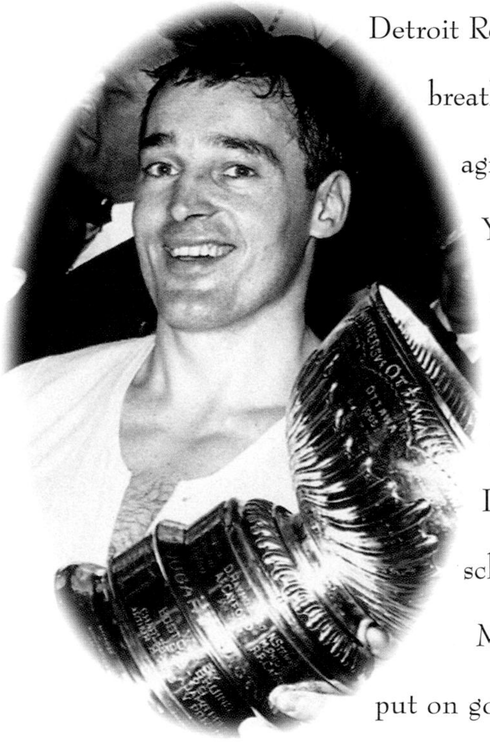

Mahovlich's arrival in the big leagues was akin to that of Bobby Orr or Eric Lindros. Everyone had tried to sign the big kid from Timmins, and the Leafs had won with cash and a scholarship to Toronto's hockey finishing school, St. Michael's College.

Mahovlich, a graceful, powerful skater with a shot that could smash Herculite, put on goal-scoring displays of such brilliance there would be a hushed and reverent pause after the puck went in the net. And yet Mahovlich, a sensitive man who liked to visit art galleries when on the road, was the target of both love and hate from Leafs fans who wanted genius all the time. He also suffered from a rocky relationship with Leafs coach Punch Imlach, who never did learn to pronounce Frank's surname correctly.

When Mahovlich, who had inspired the Leafs to four Stanley Cups, was traded to Detroit in March of 1968 in a multi-player deal that brought Norm Ullman to Toronto, the switchboard at Maple Leaf Gardens lit up in fury. Outside, stunned fans milled about, lamenting that Frank Mahovlich was untradable.

Mahovlich would star with the Red Wings and the Canadiens, and would come back to play for Toronto once more, but this time with the WHA Toros from 1974 to 1976.

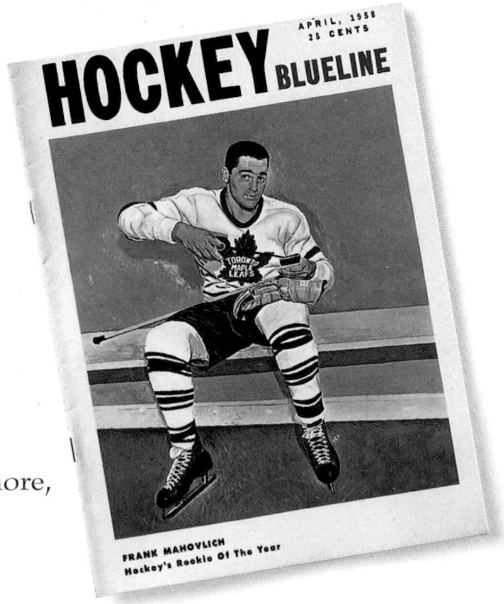

HOCKEY BLUELINE

APRIL, 1958
25 CENTS

FRANK MAHOVLICH
Hockey's Rookie Of The Year

Bill Mosienko

In an NHL speed-skating contest held at the Montreal Forum in 1950, the Chicago Blackhawks sent along "Wee Willie" Mosienko, a five-foot-eight-inch, 150-pound dynamo, and no one was surprised when he breezily beat the speedsters sent by the five other clubs.

Playing on Chicago's galloping "Pony Line" with bantamweight brothers Doug and Max Bentley, "Mosie" was known as the fastest man on skates, and the Pony Line as one of the deadliest, leading the league with 179 points in 1947–48. Three seasons before, Mosienko had won the Lady Byng Trophy, making it through the entire 1945 campaign without a single penalty and earning himself a place on the second All-Star team.

In addition to his breathtaking speed, Bill Mosienko could stickhandle like a magician, and it was this combination that led to one of the NHL's most incendiary scoring feats in New York on the night of March 23, 1952.

With the Blackhawks trailing the Rangers 6–2 and six minutes gone in the third period, Chicago sent on Mosienko with Gus Bodnar and George Gee. Bodnar won the face-off in the Rangers' zone and fed the puck to Mosienko, who swooped in on the New York goal and beat the rookie netminder with a low shot to the left.

On the next face-off, Bodnar again won the draw, snapped the puck to Mosienko, and the blindingly fast Pony was away to the races to score another goal. The line stayed on the ice to take the next face-off, and incredibly, Mosienko was once again flying solo towards the New York goal. He faked the goalie low, then went upstairs to put the puck into the top left-hand corner. Minutes later, Mosienko hit the post, narrowly missing his fourth goal, but his record-setting achievement of three goals in 21 seconds would lead the Blackhawks to a 7–6 victory over the Rangers, and ensure that the unfortunate New York goalie never played another NHL game.

Right: Madison Square Garden ticket stub from Mosienko's historic night.

Facing Page: Chicago jersey, circa 1950, complements Mosienko's game stick and 29th, 30th and 31st goal pucks – all recorded during an amazing 21-second span in the third period of the final game of the 1952 season. Mosienko would finish the year as the league's seventh best point-getter.

Jacques Plante

Jacques Plante, hockey's philosopher goaltender, won seven Vezina Trophies, six Stanley Cups and one Hart Trophy in his 19 years as a pro. He was one of the most well-travelled men in hockey, variously sporting the colours of Montreal, New York, Toronto, St. Louis and Boston, as well as the orange, white and blue of the WHA Edmonton Oilers.

Plante wore a toque in goal, knit to relax, stayed in a separate hotel from the team, and brought the age of the roving goalie to hockey. He was a private man off the ice but an exuberant showman during games. His heart-stopping voyages out of the net were a legacy of his Quebec junior hockey days, when his lead-footed teammates forced him to "go and get the puck because the defence couldn't get there fast enough." In 19 years of professional play, Plante was caught out of the net for goals only six times.

Still, the NHL Board of Governors didn't like it and passed a rule in 1959 forbidding goalies to fall on the puck while it was out of the crease. Montreal coach Toe Blake was furious, saying the Detroit Red Wings were behind the perfidy. The Wings liked to shoot the puck off the boards behind the net and quickly convert the rebound into a goal, and Plante's wanderings foiled them.

Blake was annoyed again when Plante donned a mask in a November 1, 1959, game against the Rangers after being whacked in the face in the first period. But when the Habs went on an 18-game unbeaten streak, Blake calmed down and allowed Plante to keep his mask.

From that day on, Jacques Plante, who had developed and used masks in practices, revolutionized the NHL by becoming the first goaltender to regularly use a mask in games. When someone who'd never played goal asked him, "Doesn't the mask prove you're scared?" Plante replied, "If you jumped out of a plane without a parachute, would that make you brave?"

Right: After five successive Vezina trophies and corresponding Stanley Cups, Plante was awarded his "own" Vezina in 1960 by the NHL.

Facing Page: Plante won the Stanley Cup and the Vezina Trophy the same year he debuted this original mask– 1959 (top left corner). His battered 1956–59 clear practice mask (right), his 1965 mask (bottom), and 1969 mask (top), complete the circle.

Maurice Richard

Three days after Christmas 1944, Maurice "Rocket" Richard hefted furniture—including a piano—into his new house. That night he potted five goals and three assists to lead Montreal to a 9–1 walloping of the Red Wings, setting an NHL record to boot.

During Game Seven of the 1952 Stanley Cup final against Boston, a dazed Richard, having earlier been knocked unconscious and now squinting through blood, scored the tie-breaking, Cup-winning goal. He received a four-minute standing ovation—the longest in Forum history.

Richard, a mercurial, goal-scoring genius, was like a man possessed on ice. Goalie Glenn Hall said years later, "When he was coming down on you, his eyes were flashing and gleaming like the lights of a pinball machine. It was frightening."

Richard's passion often led to conflict, and once, in what some have called the flash point for Quebec's Quiet Revolution, to a riot. On March 16, 1955, in the fury of a tempestuous game, gloves were dropped and in the ensuing melée Richard punched a linesman. President Clarence Campbell suspended Richard for the rest of the season.

Montreal fans went wild the next night when Campbell dared to show up at the game. After a tear-gas bomb exploded near Campbell, the game was forfeited to Detroit, and the violent mob rampaged down St. Catherine's Street. A devastated and bitter Richard lost the scoring title for that season by one point.

Yet despite missing many games due to injuries over his 18-year career, The Rocket scored 544 goals; won the Hart Trophy, and eight Stanley Cups; was named Canada's male athlete of the year twice; and crowned all by becoming the first player to score 50 goals in 50 games. When Montreal's *La Presse* newspaper conducted its 100th anniversary poll for the man of the century in 1983, readers responded with two names—Quebec folksinger Felix Leclerc, and Maurice "Rocket" Richard.

Right: *Richard's eyes, flashing and gleaming, stare back from* Hockey Blueline's *September 1956 cover.*

Facing Page: *The "Rocket's" legendary "number nine" game jersey, circa 1956, provides the backdrop for his 325th NHL goal stick, November 8, 1952. This milestone surpassed Nels Stewart's 324 goals, making Richard the NHL's all-time goal scorer. Parkhurst's 1953–54 trading card series celebrated Richard's greatness.*

Terry Sawchuk

When the goalie for Terry Sawchuk's bantam Winnipeg team left for balmier climes, Sawchuk—previously a star centre—was put in the net because he had goalie pads at home. The pads had belonged to his older brother, who had died of a heart ailment. As Sawchuk remembered: "The pads were there where I could always look at them…The day they put me in the net I had a good game. I've stayed there since." It would be a bittersweet foreshadowing of Sawchuk's professional career.

Bad luck and portentous omens followed Sawchuk with a kind of cruel irony: at 18, while playing for Omaha, Sawchuk took a stick in the eye. His eye was saved only because an excellent eye surgeon happened to be passing through town. On the day Hall of Fame goalie George Hainsworth was killed in a car accident, Sawchuk was starting his second game in the nets for Detroit. He would surpass Hainsworth's record of 94 NHL shutouts 11 years later.

Weeks after being banished to L.A. in the 1967 expansion draft, Sawchuk was voted the Maple Leafs most valuable player of the season.

"Suitcase" Sawchuk, who strapped on the pads for Detroit, Boston, Toronto, Los Angeles and New York, played 971 games in 21 seasons and scored 103 shutouts, more of each than any other NHL goalie. He brought the crouch position permanently into the game, and was the first player to win the rookie-of-the-year award in three leagues: the U.S. Hockey League, the AHL and the NHL. He won the Vezina Trophy three times, sharing the last one with Johnny Bower. In 1952, Sawchuk led the Detroit Red Wings to the Stanley Cup in an astonishing eight games, posting four shutouts and allowing only five goals.

The temperamental athlete whom Emile Francis called "the greatest goaltender in hockey," died in May 1970 of internal injuries sustained in an off-ice accident. Like his talented older brother, Terry Sawchuk died too young.

Right: Pucks representing the NHL travels of Sawchuk, who backstopped five different teams from 1949 to 1970.

Facing Page: Sawchuk's expressive and haunting goalie mask from his final 1969–70 season leans against his catching glove and chest protector, circa 1962, and the stick he used to record his 100th career shutout, March 4, 1967, while in the nets for the Maple Leafs.

The NHL has a long list of illustrious heroes who have provided the game with a rich and varied history. Each year the NHL awards the trophies featured here, honouring its very best by engraving contemporary names alongside those of legend. Back row, left to right: Lady Byng Memorial Trophy, awarded to the player best exhibiting sportsmanship, gentlemanly conduct and a high standard of playing ability; Vezina Trophy, for outstanding goalkeeping; Prince of Wales Trophy, to the winner of the Wales Conference championship; Stanley Cup, to the overall NHL champions; Calder Memorial Trophy, awarded to the best first year NHL player; Hart Memorial Trophy, for the most valuable regular season player; Clarence S. Campbell Bowl, to the winner of the Campbell Conference championship; Bill Masterton Memorial Trophy, to the NHL player best exemplifying perseverance, sportsmanship and dedication to hockey; Art Ross Trophy, to the leading point scorer at the end of the regular season. Front row, left to right: Frank J. Selke Trophy, to the best defensive forward; King Clancy Memorial Trophy, to the player best exemplifying leadership qualities and humanitarian contribution in his community; Lord Stanley of Preston's original 1893 challenge cup; James Norris Memorial Trophy, to the defenseman who demonstrates throughout the season the greatest all-round ability; Conn Smythe Trophy, to the most valuable player in the playoffs; William M. Jennings Award, to the goalkeeper(s) having played a minimum of 25 games for the team with the fewest goals scored against it.

C H A P T E R   S I X

1 9 6 7   1 9 9 3

Expansion

Original Stanley Cup, 1893.
Left: One hundred
years later–today's
Stanley Cup, 1993.

The NHL gave itself a 50th birthday present in 1967 when it added a half-dozen teams to the "Original Six." The "growth industry" possibilities for hockey had been debated by league officials throughout the '60s, but the young guard among owners and would-be owners knew exactly what the aggressive marketing of the National Football League and the National Basketball Association meant: competition. The scramble to fill seats was going to reach an intensity not yet seen in professional sports, and "expansion" could no longer be merely a topic of debate.

Outside the windows of the NHL boardroom, the planet was

The Avco World Trophy.

The World Hockey Association

Following the rebellious tradition of the upstart American football and basketball leagues in the 1960s, the World Hockey Association hung out its shingle in November 1971, immediately luring away NHL talent–and eventually legends like Bobby Hull and Gordie Howe–with the promise of ice surfaced with gold. The first 10 franchises ranged far from hockey's traditional northern domain. Hockey fans could now look deep into the south to follow the fortunes of teams like the Houston Aeros and the Miami Screaming Eagles.

When Bobby Hull signed with the new league's Winnipeg Jets in 1972 for a mind-boggling $2.75 million, the NHL owners declared war, obtaining an injunction forbidding Hull to play for the Jets come September because he was still the "property" of the Chicago Blackhawks. The injunction fell to pieces in a landmark court decision in October that same year, and the gate was opened for other NHL stars to skate into the WHA. Not long afterward came a wave of European players, and the complexion of North American hockey changed forever, though what remained of the WHA would merge with the NHL in 1978–79.

and goalkeeper for the Boston Bruins and Chicago Blackhawks, while Rod Gilbert, Jean Ratelle, Brad Park and Eddie Giacomin often made the Rangers the hottest ticket on Broadway. And the WHA's end saw the NHL beginning of Wayne "The Great One" Gretzky, who would go on to rewrite virtually every major NHL record.

Canadiens' legends Jean Béliveau and Toe Blake, long-serving league president Clarence Campbell and Mr. Hockey himself, Gordie Howe, all said good-bye to the game, though Howe returned to fulfill a lifelong dream by playing alongside his sons with the WHA Houston Aeros, then skated one last season in the NHL with Hartford. The NHL sadly

Norris Trophy winner and 24-year NHL veteran Harry Howell's skate, circa 1973.

lost the great Leaf and Sabre defenceman Tim Horton in a car accident, while Bill Masterton of the Minnesota North Stars died of injuries suffered in a January 1968 game and is commemorated through the Bill Masterton Memorial Trophy.

The 1980s saw a concentration of hockey brilliance that had previously been the sole domain of the Original Six. Mike Bossy and Denis Potvin powered the New York Islanders to four Stanley Cups in a row, the first American team to do so and only the third team in NHL history to win four consecutive Cups. Then it was the Edmonton Oilers' turn. Inspired by Wayne Gretzky and marshalled by Mark Messier, Grant Fuhr and Paul Coffey, the Oilers took five Cups over seven years, establishing the team as the great dynasty of the late 1980s. Closing out the decade, the "Trade of the Century" brought Wayne Gretzky to Hollywood on August 9, 1988, elevating hockey heavenward in the City of Angels.

Steve Yzerman donned the colours of the Red Wings and helped restore dignity and a winning tradition to a once great but tarnished franchise. Bobby Hull's son Brett took up dad's mantle to become "The Golden Brett" and revive the sagging Spirit of St. Louis. The aspirations of the ailing Pittsburgh Penguins were placed on the young shoulders of Mario Lemieux, and the Montreal native regularly displayed that his surname does mean "the best," marching the Penguins to two successive Cups in 1991 and 1992.

On the west coast, the San Jose Sharks were bringing hockey back once more to the Bay Area in the NHL's most recent expansion. With a regularly sold-out rink and wildly popular team merchandise, the team looked as if its cruise through NHL shoals would be much longer than its predecessors, the Seals. Lightning struck in Florida with the addition of Tampa Bay to the roster in 1992, bringing the game further south than General Sherman had ever marched, and a noble hockey tradition was revived in Ottawa with the appointment of the Senators in the same year. The famous—and in Quebec, infamous—Eric Lindros finally resolved his contretemps with the Nordiques to lend his rugged gifts to the Philadelphia Flyers.

Shortly before Christmas, the NHL gave itself an early present by confirming former National Basketball Association commissioner and TV marketing wizard Gary Bettman as NHL president, then announced that the powerful Disney and Blockbuster Entertainment corporations would be sponsoring teams in Anaheim and Miami. Just as it had in 1967, the NHL was going after the teeming metropolitan markets it needed to put the game on prime time and fully into the North American sports consciousness. Once more the NHL was taking a promising—and necessary—step forward.

Canadian astronaut Marc Garneau carried this NHL puck into space in 1985.

Wayne Gretzky

Once—maybe once—in a generation an athlete appears who is so talented that previous gauges of excellence have to be recalibrated to understand the magnitude of that talent.

Wayne Gretzky is such an athlete. He rewrote the record books as both an Edmonton Oiler and Los Angeles King to become outright owner of 30 NHL individual records. One of these was most points by a player in the recorded history of hockey, which he achieved by surpassing Gordie Howe's total of 1,850 points on October 15, 1989, in Edmonton.

"The Great One" has so far won virtually every NHL award for which he is eligible, among them some of the most coveted trophies in the game: the Hart Trophy as the NHL's most valuable player nine times; the Art Ross Trophy as the NHL's leading scorer nine times; the Lady Byng Trophy three times; the Conn Smythe twice; and five Stanley Cups as the crown jewel of the Edmonton Oilers dynasty in the 1980s. Now playing as a Los Angeles King, Gretzky still dominates as one of the game's great geniuses, his career an icon of professional sport.

Two-year-old Wayne Gretzky took the first steps of his celebrated career on these skates, circa 1963.

Bobby Clarke

Even though Bobby Clarke had burned up the Western Canada Junior Hockey League with 137 points as he led the Flin Flon Bombers to "win the West," the dauntless centre was selected 17th in the 1969 amateur draft. Only Philadelphia Flyers owner Ed Snider and general manager Keith Allen would take a chance when no one else would: Clarke was diabetic, and managerial wisdom felt that while he might be a star with the kids, Clarke's formidable will and daily insulin injections would not be enough in the gruelling, big-game world of the NHL.

Clarke would prove the greybeards embarrassingly wrong over the next 15 years, taking on the NHL with the same grit he had shown in the juniors and winning the Masterton, Pearson, Patrick and Selke trophies; the Hart Trophy three times; the Stanley Cup twice; and in 1975, the Lou Marsh Trophy as Canada's Athlete of the Year.

In the 1972–73 season, Clarke, famed for his mop of hair and toothless grin, became the first expansion-team player to record a 100-point season. Though only 23, Clarke was the heart of the soaring Flyers and was appointed captain by coach Fred Shero.

The following year in the Stanley Cup finals, Clarke showed just how impenetrable his will to win was. The Flyers had only beaten the Bruins four times in 38 games, and not at all in their last 18 visits to Boston. After losing Game One to the Bruins in Boston, "The Broad Street Bullies" found themselves down 2–0 in Game Two. Bobby Clarke, playing as if his life depended on this game, began the Flyers' astonishing comeback by scoring one unanswered goal, then, with only 52 seconds on the clock, another. Twelve minutes into sudden-death overtime, Clarke potted his third to beat the Bruins and pull the series even. The victory gave Philadelphia the momentum to become the first 1967 expansion team to win the Stanley Cup.

Right:
Clarke's "heart and soul" cover story, Hockey Illustrated, *March 1975.*

Facing Page:
"Taking the most direct route to the puck," Clarke led the Flyers by example for 15 seasons. His captain's jersey, circa 1970s, in company with a collection of notable game sticks, left to right: Soviet series, 1976; 116th point, 1975; 250th goal, 1978; 119th point, 1976; and 350th goal, 1983–84 season.

Marcel Dionne

When Marcel Dionne was a child playing midget hockey in Quebec, he was already a star. People would thrust programs and scraps of paper at young Dionne to autograph, but he was barely able to reach over the boards to sign them.

By the time he reached the NHL, Dionne was still only five feet seven inches tall, but his nickname "Little Beaver" was a nod to his compact stature and a reference to the ring moniker of a midget wrestler. It was appropriate because Dionne had turned into a battling, whirling, goal-scoring dervish. Selected second overall in the 1971 amateur draft by the Detroit Red Wings, he scored 366 points in his first four seasons with Detroit—more points in a four-year period than Rocket Richard, Gordie Howe, Bobby Orr, Phil Esposito, Bobby Hull or any other player in NHL history.

Though Dionne's game was so elegant and clean it twice won him the Lady Byng Trophy for gentlemanly play, his off-ice frustrations sometimes became very public, much to management's chagrin. When the Little Beaver couldn't prove his point with the puck, he would at times resort to incendiary displays of temper. Both Dionne and the Wings eventually wearied of their rumbles, and so he was traded to the Los Angeles Kings on June 23, 1975.

Dionne glinted in the California sun, becoming the jewel in the Kings' "Triple Crown Line" with Dave Taylor and Charlie Simmer. Oddly enough, Dionne's success in the land of surf and palm trees prompted some to suggest he was avoiding his Quebeçois destiny: to play for the Montreal Canadiens and lead them once more to the promised land. Dionne's response on ice was regal, as his play under the purple and gold of the Kings won him the Art Ross Trophy as the league's leading scorer, another Lady Byng Trophy and, in spite of those who wanted him in Montreal's colours, a place in hockey legend as the leading French-Canadian goal scorer in NHL history.

Ken Dryden

There have been other scholar-athletes, but Ken Dryden was different, possessing a transcendental detachment as he made his extraordinary saves in net for the Montreal Canadiens.

Having starred in goal for Cornell University, Dryden moved home to Canada and McGill Law School and backstopped the Montreal Voyageurs. In the spring of 1971, the rangy six-foot-four-inch Dryden was called up to the Canadiens. He became an instant icon: "The Thinker," resting on his stick after robbing yet another marksman of a seemingly sure goal. Dryden's magical Stanley Cup series against Chicago would stretch seven games and win him the Conn Smythe Trophy as the most valuable player on the ice.

From 1971 to 1979, Ken Dryden astonished players and fans alike with goaltending that created order out of chaos, stopping pucks with an amazing grace that seemed to defy the laws of physics. Honours naturally followed: the Calder Trophy; five Vezina Trophies; and six more Cups for the Montreal Canadiens.

Dryden, who would pursue a post-hockey career as a lawyer and author, explained in his fine book *The Game* that, like others before him, he probably became a goalie because his older brother Dave was one. Young Ken got both his older brother's equipment and a heroic figure to emulate.

On the night of March 2, 1971, the brothers Dryden made hockey history when fate helped them become the first siblings to face each other in NHL nets. After an injury removed Rogie Vachon, Ken Dryden skated into the nets for the Habs. Buffalo coach Punch Imlach immediately sent Dave Dryden into goal, and the Forum broke into applause, appreciating Imlach's grand gesture. Though Montreal would win 5–2, the Dryden brothers each allowed only two goals and at the end of the game did something only seen in Stanley Cup play-offs—they skated to centre ice and shook hands, thus completing the circle of a childhood desire.

Right:
The 1972 Summit Series saw Dryden star behind this mask, which he wore from 1970 to 1973.

Facing Page:
Dryden's red, white and blue practice mask, circa 1975, nestles between his skates, pads and stick, circa 1978–79. During his seven-year tenure as the NHL's premier goaltender, Dryden never lost more than 10 games in a season, averaging 56 games per year, not including play-offs.

Phil Esposito

Phil Esposito didn't take up skating until he was a teen, and his shaky skills helped keep the 18-year-old Sault Ste. Marie native from making the St. Catherine's Junior "A" team, the farm club of the Chicago Blackhawks. Instead, the future winner of the Art Ross Trophy took $15 a week and a spot on the bench for a Junior "B" club in Sarnia. Esposito made the St. Catherine's team the following year, but his shot at the NHL was a long one.

The Chicago Blackhawks finally took a chance on Esposito in 1963, and though he scored 74 goals over the next four seasons, the Hawks got reckless in 1967: they dealt Ken Hodge, Wayne Stanfield and Phil Esposito to the Bruins. It was a trade the Hawks would live to regret.

Boston brought out the best in Phil Esposito: he became the first NHLer to break the 100-point barrier, going on to five league scoring titles in his eight and a half seasons with the Bruins. Esposito's deadly eye and his ability to remain on his skates even when buffeted by heavy defensive turbulence, helped him put the puck in the net forwards, backwards, shorthanded, single-handed, two-handed and either-handed.

"Espo" scored 55 goals or more in five consecutive seasons and became the fastest man to reach 500 goals, hitting the mark in 803 games—60 faster than record-holder Rocket Richard.

The passionate Esposito led the Bruins to two Stanley Cups, and, after an emotional rinkside plea in Vancouver to wavering Canadian fans, inspired Team Canada to victory over the Soviets in the 1972 Series of the Century. This two-time winner of the Hart Trophy, the man who nearly didn't make it to the NHL, was twice voted the Lester B. Pearson Award by the NHL Players' Association as their most valuable player, won the Lester Patrick Award for his contribution to hockey in the U.S., and was made an Officer of the Order of Canada.

Right: *Esposito's last NHL point, scored as a Ranger, was with this puck, January 9, 1981.*

Facing Page: *Esposito's arsenal of milestone sticks supports his record-breaking 98th-point puck and stick from March 1, 1969. After smashing the NHL record for most points in a season, previously held by Bobby Hull and Stan Mikita, Esposito would go on to set a modern-day record of 126 points.*

Eddie Giacomin

Eddie Giacomin never seemed to get an even break. He was cut from a Detroit Junior "A" tryout when he was 15. When he showed up at the Red Wings camp at 18, he was sent home. Giacomin went back to Sudbury but didn't give up, instead playing two seasons in an industrial league. In 1959, the man nicknamed "Go-Go" because of his wandering netminding style got a break: his brother Rollie was asked to play for the Washington (D.C.) Presidents of the Eastern Hockey League. Rollie couldn't go, so Eddie went instead and played so well he was invited to the American Hockey League's Providence Reds training camp.

And then trouble literally exploded when a kitchen stove blew up in Giacomin's face. Suffering second-and third-degree burns to his legs and feet, he was told he'd never play hockey again. After a year spent with his legs in bandages, the unsinkable Giacomin returned and performed so well he was given a shot at the "show" by New York Rangers coach Emile Francis.

The streetsmart Rangers' fans adored Giacomin's flashy style and chanted "Ed-die, Ed-die" whenever he made a particularly acrobatic save. In his decade with New York, Giacomin shared the Vezina, won 226 games, and posted more shutouts than any goalie in team history, but in November 1975, the Rangers made a tactical error: they sold Giacomin to the Detroit Red Wings two days before the Wings were to play in New York. When Eddie Giacomin skated out in a Red Wing jersey, Ranger fans gave him a deafening roar of welcome, while former teammates apologized for any goals they might score on him. And when the game began, an astonishing thing happened: Ranger fans booed the home team and cheered their beloved Giacomin. That night, he would score one more emotional victory in Madison Square Garden, as he backstopped the Wings to a 6–4 victory and garnered a standing ovation of farewell.

Right: Giacomin starred in O-Pee-Chee's 1971–72 mini hockey booklet.

Facing Page: Giacomin's acrobatic style earned him a lifetime 2.82 goals-against average, which he achieved donning the pads for the Rangers and the Red Wings. Giacomin's stacked pads, circa 1977–78, support his blocker, jersey and glove, circa 1977–78, and his mask and 50th-shutout stick, both originating from the 1975–76 campaign.

Rod Gilbert

New York Rangers marksman Rod Gilbert was one of the most flawless skaters to wear the Broadway Blueshirts' colours, yet he was nearly crippled as a Guelph junior when his skate caught on a some rubbish thrown onto the ice. Gilbert crashed so heavily he broke his back and nearly lost a leg during two spinal fusion operations. He philosophically considered the fact that he could skate at all to be the "one big thrill" of his career.

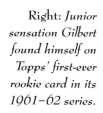

Gilbert was a virtual thrill factory, stickhandling with such finesse and shooting with such scorching accuracy that when he retired after 18 seasons with the Rangers, he held or shared team records in 23 categories, including most regular season goals (406); most play-off goals (34); and most regular season assists (615). And with 1,021 regular season points, he was second only to Gordie Howe.

Ironically, Gilbert's best season came after a dispute with Rangers' management in 1972. Gilbert asked general manager Emile Francis for a raise from $53,000 a season to $75,000. Bobby Hull was making $100,000 a year, and the Rangers' star figured he was "three quarters as good" as the Golden Jet. Francis nodded, pondered, then countered with a meagre $2,000 bonus. The disagreement went before an arbitrator.

Gilbert prepared his 22-page brief himself. The arbitrator scanned it, then asked Gilbert to leave the room as Francis stayed behind. When Gilbert was summoned back, the arbitrator informed him he was awarding him $53,000 – his original salary.

Gilbert responded by scoring 43 goals and 54 assists on a line with Jean Ratelle and Vic Hadfield, and making the first All-Star team. Rangers president William Jennings, not about to make the same mistake twice, persuaded Gilbert not to jump to the WHA by giving him a $150,000 raise. Gilbert stayed, going on to win the Bill Masterton Memorial Trophy as the player best exemplifying the "qualities of perseverance, sportsmanship and dedication to hockey."

Right: Junior sensation Gilbert found himself on Topps' first-ever rookie card in its 1961–62 series.

Facing Page: En route to setting or equalling 20 Ranger records, Gilbert fired his 43rd goal with this stick, circa 1971–72, a career high tally. Gilbert's jersey, circa 1976, and souvenir puck are reminders of the single season the Rangers abandoned their classic jerseys for a chevron-inspired replacement.

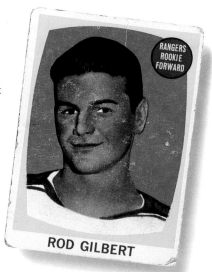

ROD GILBERT

Guy Lafleur

Guy Lafleur's arrival in the NHL was heralded as the passing of the torch. Jean Beliveau retired that year and offered the young Thurso, Quebec, star his number 4 jersey, the number Lafleur had worn while burning up the Quebec Junior League with 209 points in two seasons. The humble Lafleur graciously declined and instead immortalized number 10 over his 13½ seasons as a Hab to become the greatest goal-scorer in the history of a franchise rich with goal-scoring genius.

"The Flower" was such a subtle combination of balletic grace and transcendent power that fans in rinks around the NHL came just to see him play. He was the first to score 50 goals in six consecutive seasons, and the first to have six straight 100-point seasons. He was also the youngest player in history to score 400 goals, and the youngest to reach 1,000 points. Lafleur's reaction to this was characteristically practical: "I'm not going to say that now I have 1,000 points I can sit down and relax. I've got five or six more years to go so I can shoot for more." Lafleur was no aloof superstar but very much a man of the people. When the Canadiens won the Stanley Cup in 1978, Lafleur "borrowed" Lord Stanley's legacy, and took it home to Thurso. People came from near and far to see hockey's fabled trophy standing on the Lafleurs' front lawn.

Three seasons after retiring from the Habs, Lafleur joined the New York Rangers in 1988. Following a season with the Rangers he came home to wear the blue-and-white fleur-de-lis of the Quebec Nordiques. When Lafleur, who was elected to the Hockey Hall of Fame in 1988, finally closed his glorious career in 1992, the Nordiques honoured him with an emotional farewell at La Colisée. His message was fitting for a man who had redefined the concept of hockey excellence: "Play every game," said The Flower, "as if it were your last."

Right: A ticket for the record books: Lafleur's 500th goal, December 20, 1983, scored in a game against the New Jersey Devils.

Facing Page: Lafleur's 50th-goal stick, circa 1975, crosses in front of his 43rd-goal stick, circa 1974, face-off fashion. His Canadiens jersey, circa 1979 and souvenir program, October 17, 1981, stand above a trio of O-Pee-Chee trading cards, circa 1973–81.

Lanny McDonald

When Lanny McDonald was a kid in Hannah, Alberta, the time-zone difference meant that *Hockey Night in Canada* began at 6 p.m. Young McDonald absently shovelled in his food as he watched his beloved Toronto Maple Leafs and his hero Dave Keon on TV. "I fastened my eyes on Keon—up, down, zip. Supper was all hockey."

When McDonald joined the Leafs in 1973, it was as if destiny was being fulfilled. Not only did he become Keon's right-winger, but his first NHL goal gave the Leafs their first win over their arch-rival Canadiens in the Montreal Forum in three years.

That historic goal was the first of many in McDonald's 16 seasons in the NHL. The hugely popular, walrus-mustachioed player had a shot like a cannon. When McDonald—rather callously discarded by Leafs owner Harold Ballard— eventually wound up with the Calgary Flames, coach Bob Johnson marvelled, "When he shoots, the puck just seems to go in the net."

Although a rugged, physical player, McDonald was famous for his clean play and scrupulous honesty. After scoring his 400th goal in a Flames win over Winnipeg, McDonald was bothered by a hunch that the puck might have really gone in off his teammate Eddie Beers. McDonald watched a videotape of the game at home and saw clearly that the goal wasn't his. The next day he called the NHL Official Scorer and asked that the goal be changed.

When McDonald decided to retire at the end of the 1989 season, the fates returned with beautiful symmetry. McDonald stepped on the ice after serving a penalty to score the goal that gave the Flames a 2–1 lead, a lead they would sustain to the end of the game to win the Stanley Cup. It was the last goal of his career, scored against the Montreal Canadiens and in the Forum, where McDonald had netted his first NHL goal and game winner over the Habs 16 years earlier.

Right:
McDonald's O-Pee-Chee rookie card, circa 1974–75, shows him as a clean-shaven Maple Leaf.

Facing Page:
McDonald, in this battle-worn helmet and number nine jersey, captained the Calgary Flames to their first-ever Stanley Cup in 1989. He recorded his 400th goal during the 1983–84 season with this stick, en route to scoring 544 NHL goals.

Bobby Orr

Of the 296 goals Bobby Orr scored in his brilliant career, the one that enters the realm of legend took place in the Stanley Cup final on Mother's Day, 1970. A banner high above the ice wished Orr's mother a happy one. She wouldn't be disappointed.

The Boston rink was a steaming 90°F as the upstart expansion St. Louis Blues skated out to meet the Bruins in overtime. The players, drained by the deadlock and the humidity, wanted to end this one quickly. With the puck deep in the St. Louis zone, Orr blocked a clearing pass, then slid the puck to teammate Derek Sanderson in a "give-and-go."

Sanderson placed the puck perfectly on Orr's stick, and Orr, about to go airborne courtesy of St. Louis defenceman Noel Picard, scored the game winner a mere 40 seconds into overtime to give the Bruins their first Stanley Cup victory in 29 years.

Sadly, Orr's brilliant career was truncated by increasingly debilitating knee problems. Orr once remarked that "if I were a horse they'd probably shoot me." Yet despite his dodgy knees, Orr was a pioneer: the first defenceman to score more than 40 goals in a season, win the scoring title and score more than 100 points. He was also the first player to notch more than 100 assists, the first defenceman to win the Conn Smythe Trophy, and the world's first $1-million hockey player. He won the Calder Trophy as rookie of the year, the Norris Trophy as the NHL's best defenceman eight times, the Hart thrice, the Smythe and Ross trophies twice, the Lou Marsh Trophy as Canada's top male athlete of the year, and the Lester Patrick Trophy for his contribution to hockey in the U.S. When Orr retired, the mayor of Boston said Orr had been to the city "the equivalent of a great natural resource, like Paul Revere's house or the Bunker Hill Monument. Some things cannot be replaced."

Right: A big hit with the fans, Orr's hockey wisdom was preserved on vinyl, circa 1970.

Facing Page: Harry Sinden, Orr's Boston coach, said: "Bobby was a star from the moment they played the national anthem in his first NHL game." He was right. Orr's game jersey, circa 1973, joins a foursome of game-scarred sticks, including his 200th-goal stick from the 1973–74 season.

Bernie Parent

Goaltending legend Glenn Hall once lamented that "having a goal scored against you is like having your pants taken down in front of 15,000 people." Bernie Parent was metaphorically de-panted 20 times during his first game in the nets, but the only witnesses were his other 11-year-old friends and Parent's older brother, who had hastily press-ganged young Bernie into service. The humiliating defeat only made Parent try harder, and on his next outing his team won 5–3, a goaltender was born, and Philadelphians would one day see bumper stickers declaring, "Only the Lord Saves More Than Bernie Parent."

Claimed from Boston by Philadelphia in the 1967 expansion draft, Parent backstopped the Flyers to two Stanley Cups and twice won the Conn Smythe and Vezina trophies. Like his idol Jacques Plante, Parent's style was a combination of science, instinct and staying on his skates. He was a master at playing the angles, skating out to the edge of his crease, tapping the goal posts behind him, then setting up and waiting, daring the shooter to make the first move.

One of Parent's greatest—and most bizarre—goaltending challenges came during the 1975 Stanley Cup finals against the Sabres. In Game Four on May 22, the temperature inside Buffalo's arena seemed to be over 100°F, creating a soupy fog just off the ice. Parent said that trying to stop shots by Buffalo's deadly "French Connection Line" of Perrault, Martin and Robert was hard enough at the best of times, "but having them wear white sweaters and shoot at you through fog was a good way to wind up in the hospital."

Parent saw through the haze to sip champagne from the Stanley Cup five days later. Having led the Flyers to their second straight championship with four play-off shutouts and a goals-against average of 1.89, he was deservedly awarded with the Smythe Trophy as the series' most valuable player.

Right: *Parent's last pair of game skates, inscribed with the signatures of his Philadelphia teammates, February 17, 1979.*

Facing Page: *Parent stared down the opposition from behind this mask, circa 1979, in his final NHL season. Parent's game stick, circa 1974, and Flyers souvenir puck play backup to his warlike facegear.*

Gilbert Perreault

When Gilbert Perreault was ready to enter the NHL, Bernie Geoffrion said, "You could start a franchise with him." And that's exactly what the Buffalo Sabres did. With a little bit of help from "Lady Luck."

The first choice in the 1970 expansion draft between the Sabres and the Vancouver Canucks was to be decided by the spinning of a huge roulette wheel. Sabres general manager Punch Imlach, famous for his superstitiousness, picked his favourite number—11. League president Clarence Campbell spun the wheel and announced that it had stopped at number 1. As the Canucks' delegation whooped, the canny Imlach took a closer look and saw that the wheel actually showed number 11. Gilbert Perreault was now a Buffalo Sabre.

Over the next 18 seasons, "franchise builder" Perreault would repeatedly prove the truth of Geoffrion's prophecy, winning both the Calder and Byng trophies, and racking up 1,326 points in 1,191 games as the centrepiece of Buffalo's dreaded "French Connection Line." Perreault's raw skating and shooting power as well as his stickhandling finesse was a potent combination. He also seemed to have the ability to go in three directions at once, moving Bobby Orr to marvel, "His head and shoulders go one way, his legs go the other way, and the puck is doing something else. When I first saw it I couldn't believe it."

Hall of Fame referee Frank Udvari—a veteran of nearly 800 NHL games—couldn't believe it either. "I have never seen a player deke so many players out of their underwear—he made even the big players look ordinary in the All-Star game."

When Perreault hung up his skates for good at the end of the 1987–88 season, he became the first Buffalo Sabre to have his number taken out of service. Buffalo preserved Perreault's great legacy for future generations of Sabres by retiring the number that won him—Punch Imlach's lucky number 11.

Right: Puck from Perreault and fellow Sabres' home opener against the Montreal Canadiens, October 15, 1970.

Facing Page: A silver-plated sabre commemorating Buffalo's NHL entry duels with a half dozen of Perreault's "milestone" sticks. Left to right: 30 goals, 1974-75; 400th goal, 1982-83; 113th point, 1975-76; 106th point, 1978-79; 350th goal, 1980-81; and his 35th rookie goal, 1970-71 season.

Denis Potvin

Called "the second Bobby Orr" when he dazzled as a 14-year-old Ottawa junior hockey player, Denis Potvin was the rock upon which the New York Islanders built their franchise and their dynasty of the 1980s.

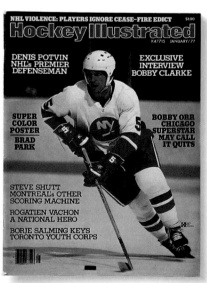

"The Bear's" uncommon strength, fearless hitting and offensive gifts won him the Calder Trophy as the league's top rookie in 1974, the Norris Trophy as the NHL's best defenceman three times, and led the powerful Islanders to four consecutive Stanley Cups.

Potvin was one of the last great hip-checkers, using his six-foot, 200-pound frame to throw devastating checks at freewheeling forwards who had thought the technique a relic of a bygone era. He not only captained the Islanders' team but also their offence, using his intelligence and patience to set up effective power plays from his spot on the left point.

The supremely confident defenceman often appeared arrogant. And although he was one of the luminaries on the 1976 and 1981 Canada Cup teams, Potvin further provoked those who would dismiss him as an uppity parvenu by publicly saying that he, not Bobby Orr, should have won the 1976 "most valuable player" award. Yet that direct style of self-confidence was also the quality that won Potvin the deep respect of his opponents and gave the New York Islanders the will to dominate the league in a way only two teams had done before.

When Potvin retired in 1988 with "nothing left to prove" after 15 seasons as an Islander, he had broken Bobby Orr's goal-scoring and points records and had racked up the most goals (310), assists (742) and points (1,052) for an NHL defenceman. In a tribute that left the articulate Potvin without words, the Ottawa 67s, Potvin's junior team, raised his junior jersey to the roof to hang as a symbol of hockey excellence.

Right: The January 1977 edition of Hockey Illustrated *heralded Potvin as the NHL's premier defenceman, while featuring Brad Park and Bobby Orr in the same issue.*

Facing Page: A monument to his rookie season, the Calder Trophy Potvin won in 1974 is teamed with his Islander jersey, circa 1984, and autographed 300th-goal stick from the 1987–88 campaign– Potvin's final season.

Darryl Sittler

Darryl Sittler is a classic example of the Canadian hero, a poor kid from a small Ontario town who, through hard work and perseverance, became one of the Toronto Maple Leafs' greatest centres. As former Leaf and Vancouver Canuck star Tiger Williams once said: "Guy Lafleur is big in Quebec, but in Saskatchewan he can't compare to Darryl Sittler."

Sittler tempered his extraordinary athletic achievement with modesty, saying that if he hadn't made it to the NHL he would have become a crane operator like his father and been happy. He grew up in a family of eight where money had to be stretched a long way. His first pair of skates came from a neighbour whose son—future NHLer Rod Seiling—had outgrown them. The skates were gratefully accepted if a little tight, so Sittler wore them without socks—a practice he continued throughout his 13 years in the NHL.

Darryl Sittler reached "goaltender's nightmare" status on February 7, 1976, when he fired in six goals, set up four more to lead the Leafs to an 11–4 shellacking of the Boston Bruins, and beat Rocket Richard's 1944 game record of five goals and three assists.

But Sittler wasn't finished. He went on to score five goals in a play-off game against the Philadelphia Flyers, then crowned the year with the game-and series-winning goal against Czechoslovakia in the first Canada Cup, a goal Sittler called "the biggest of my life."

Yet Sittler's goal-scoring prowess came after reaching the NHL. He'd stay late after practice to work on his puckhandling skills with more accomplished teammates, and his legendary stamina often meant practising with Sittler was more draining than a regular team workout.

The hard-way/hard-work method paid rich dividends. Captain Sittler left the Leafs as their all-time leading scorer with 389 goals, their second-place leader in assists with 527, and the first Leaf during the team's long and distinguished history to score 100 points in a season.

Right:
O-Pee-Chee's 1970 rookie trading card series introduced a 20-year-old Darryl Sittler.

Facing Page:
"Every time I had the puck, something seemed to happen," said the 25-year-old Sittler with a smile after his historic night in 1976. And happen it did, as Sittler's Leaf captain jersey, circa 1975, and this team of milestone sticks (including his 250th, 300th and 350th goal) attests.

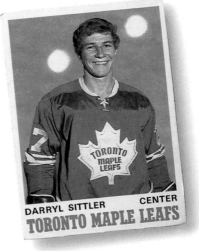

DARRYL SITTLER   CENTER
TORONTO MAPLE LEAFS

Vladislav Tretiak

The man called "the Georges Vezina of the Soviet Union" first burned himself into the North American consciousness in the 1972 Summit Series between Canada and the U.S.S.R. It scarcely seemed possible that the wraithlike 20-year-old netminder wearing what looked like a catcher's mask could keep defying the odds with such brilliant saves.

Even before the series the NHL scouts had written him off as a sieve, and as Tretiak explained with great amusement years later, the unwitting scouts had seen him play in a practice session when he definitely had other things on his mind. "I was supposed to get married, but due to the series I had to postpone the wedding three times and that wasn't easy. There were lots of other guys who wanted to marry my wife too."

Tretiak was married on August 23rd. Two days later he was back in training and a day after that the team left for Canada. "I tell people I spent my honeymoon with Canadian players."

Even so, the emotionally beleaguered Tretiak reminded Canadian players of the greatest of the NHL greats. Paul Henderson, the goalie's nemesis in the 1972 series, said, "I've seen him stop the best of them. I always said Sawchuk was one of the best I've seen. If there is a comparison to an NHL goalie I would make for Tretiak, it would be to Sawchuk."

Yet the gracious, affable Tretiak, who in 1978 won the Order of Lenin, never fulfilled his fondest wish: to play in the NHL. After having his epaulettes ripped off by the Soviet authorities when he dared suggest on a North American tour that he would like to play for the Montreal Canadiens, Tretiak was forced to say he had been misquoted by western journalists. He would later set the record straight, saying, a touch wistfully, "I was not telling the truth. I would have loved to play in Montreal. That is my city."

Right: Tickets were in demand when Tretiak toured the NHL in 1976 and again in 1979.

Facing Page: Truly an international legend, Tretiak wore this Soviet jersey during the 1972 Summit Series. He would go on to win 10 world titles and three Olympic golds before retiring in 1985. Souvenir autographed stick and commemorative card accompany Tretiak's number 20.

Epilogue

When the game of hockey took its first choppy strides on frozen Canadian ponds, with stripped tree branches serving as sticks and "horse apples" functioning as crude pucks, its players could scarcely have imagined how over the next two centuries the game would grow into a sophisticated international sport, firing up our imaginations through the coldest days of winter. Those early players, who were slowly but surely beginning to invent the game as we know it, could only have dreamed that someday hockey would produce players of such genius that their athletic feats would be elevated to legend and they would be enshrined in the Hockey Hall of Fame.

As the children of each new generation take their first tentative steps on the ice, leaning on their sticks for support, swiping optimistically at the puck and learning how to get up again after a bruising tumble, they can dream of one day taking their place in the pantheon of hockey legends. Even the youngest and humblest of skaters feels invincible when gliding down the ice faster than they've ever gone, the wind rushing by like the roar of the crowd, and all the world their rink, alive with infinite possibility. Maybe, with a lucky bounce or two of the puck, the young skater will grow up to win a place alongside those Hockey Hall of Fame legends whose years of glory, triumph and sometimes heartbreak are found in this book. Yet such is the power of the game of hockey that in the province of their imaginations, the young skaters are already there.

More than 40 of the world's countries have discovered the joy of lacing up the skates, to learn and love the game on ice. To meet the brave new frontier at which hockey finds itself as the century draws to a close, the Hockey Hall of Fame has moved into a building worthy of the honoured members it enshrines and the global game it celebrates.

The Latin inscription above the 1885 historical bank building at the corner of Toronto's Yonge and Front streets offers the visitor "Concordia" and "Salus," and it is indeed a welcoming harmony that characterizes the beautifully renovated bank, home to more than one hundred years' worth of hockey treasures. With 51,000 square feet of space at its disposal, the Hockey Hall of Fame has created an entertaining and educational tribute to hockey excellence and imbued it with a love of the game.

With displays chronicling and re-creating the history of ice hockey, to those using state-of-the-art, interactive technology that allows guests access to hockey information from around the globe, the Hockey Hall of Fame provides a rich and inspiring perspective on one of the world's fastest team sports. Crowning all is the superbly restored Great Hall. Here hockey's most illustrious trophies, including North America's oldest competitive sports trophy, the Stanley Cup, are housed under a stained-glass dome that features the crests of Canada's first eight provinces.

The Hockey Hall of Fame is a shrine to both the history and the continuing development of one of the world's favourite games. And in the tradition of shrines, the building and its contents take on a life of their own, one that merges with those of its guests to create a magnificent universe not found on any map. For as long as we

wish, we can journey through the luminous world of honoured members who once upon a time lit up the ice with their passion and their excellence. Or we can tour the galaxy of current stars whose splendour continues to make the Hockey Hall of Fame fluid and vital. Like the stories and treasures of the hockey legends revealed in this book, the game and its shrine are gloriously alive, bounded only by our ability to imagine.

Members' Honour Roll

NOTE: Early hockey statistics are incomplete and/or unavailable prior to the formation of the National Hockey League. Statistics provided were researched from Hockey Hall of Fame archival sources including newspapers, scrapbooks and recollections of early games.

All totals are NHL, unless otherwise indicated:
*indicates non-NHL career totals.
† indicates combined NHL & non-NHL career totals.
x or —— indicates information unavailable.

RS Regular Season
PO Playoffs

Players

Player	Teams		Games Played	Goals	Assists	Total Points	Penalty Minutes
ABEL, SID Melville, Saskatchewan 1918 – Inducted 1969	Pittsburgh Hornets 1938 – 39 IAIIL Detroit Red Wings 1938 – 43 & 1945 – 52 NHL Indianapolis Capitols 1939 – 40 AHL Chicago Blackhawks 1952 – 54 NHL	RS PO	613 96	189 28	283 30	472 58	376 77
ADAMS, JACK Fort William, Ontario 1895 – 1968 Inducted 1959	Toronto Arenas 1917 – 19 NHL Vancouver Millionaires 1919 – 22 PCHA Toronto St. Pats 1922 – 26 NHL Ottawa Senators 1926 – 27 NHL	RS† PO†	243 28	134 11	50 x	184 11	307 12
APPS, SYL Paris, Ontario 1915 – Inducted 1961	Toronto Maple Leafs 1936 – 43 & 1945 – 48 NHL	RS PO	423 69	201 25	231 28	432 53	56 16
ARMSTRONG, GEORGE Skead, Ontario 1930 – Inducted 1975	Toronto Maple Leafs 1949 – 50 NHL Pittsburgh Hornets 1950 – 52 AHL Toronto Maple Leafs 1951 – 71 NHL	RS PO	1187 110	296 26	417 34	713 60	721 52
BAILEY, IRVINE "ACE" Bracebridge, Ontario 1903 – 1992 Inducted 1975	St. Mary's Juniors 1921 – 22 St. Mary's Seniors 1922 – 24 Peterborough 1924 – 26 Toronto St. Pats 1926 – 27 NHL Toronto Maple Leafs 1927 – 34 NHL	RS PO	313 20	111 3	82 4	193 7	472 12
BAIN, DAN Belleville, Ontario 1874 – 1962 Inducted 1945	Winnipeg Victorias 1895 – 1902 MHL	RS* PO*	x 11	x 10	x x	x x	x x
BAKER, HOBEY Wissahickon, Pennsylvania 1892 – 1918 Inducted 1945	St. Pauls 1908 – 09 Princeton University 1910 – 14 St. Nicholas 1914 – 15	RS PO	x x	x x	x x	x x	x x
BARBER, BILL Callander, Ontario 1952 – Inducted 1990	Richmond Robins 1972 – 73 AHL Philadelphia Flyers 1972 – 84 NHL	RS PO	903 129	420 53	463 55	883 108	623 109
BARRY, MARTY St. Gabriel, Quebec 1905 – 1969 Inducted 1965	NY Americans 1927 – 28 NHL Boston Bruins 1929 – 35 NHL Detroit Red Wings 1935 – 39 NHL Montreal Canadiens 1939 – 40 NHL	RS PO	509 43	195 15	192 18	387 33	231 34
BATHGATE, ANDY Winnipeg, Manitoba 1932 – Inducted 1978	NY Rangers 1952 – 64 NHL Vancouver Cancuks 1952 – 54 & 1968 – 70 WHL Cleveland Barons 1953 – 54 AHL Toronto Maple Leafs 1963 – 65 NHL Detroit Red Wings 1965 – 67 NHL Pittsburgh Hornets 1966 – 67 AHL Pittsburgh Penguins 1967 – 68 & 1970 – 71 NHL Vancouver Blazers 1974 – 75 WHA	RS PO	1069 54	349 21	624 14	973 35	624 76
BÉLIVEAU, JEAN Trois Rivières, Quebec 1931 – Inducted 1972	Montreal Canadiens 1950 – 51 & 1952 – 71 NHL Quebec Aces 1951 – 53 QHL	RS PO	1125 162	507 79	712 97	1219 176	1029 211
BENTLEY, DOUG Delisle, Saskatchewan 1916 – 1972 Inducted 1964	Chicago Blackhawks 1939 – 44 & 1945 – 52 NHL Saskatoon Quakers 1951 – 54 WHL NY Rangers 1953 – 54 NHL	RS PO	566 23	219 9	324 8	543 17	217 12
BENTLEY, MAX Delisle, Saskatchewan 1920 – 1984 Inducted 1966	Chicago Blackhawks 1940 – 43 & 1945 – 48 NHL Toronto Maple Leafs 1947 – 53 NHL NY Rangers 1953 – 54 NHL	RS PO	646 52	245 18	299 27	544 45	175 14
BLAKE, HECTOR "TOE" Victoria Mines, Ontario 1912 – Inducted 1966	Montreal Maroons 1934 – 35 NHL Providence Reds 1935 – 36 CAHL Montreal Canadiens 1935 – 48 NHL	RS PO	578 57	235 25	292 37	527 62	272 23
BOIVIN, LEO Prescott, Ontario 1932 – Inducted 1986	Pittsburgh Hornets 1951 – 52 AHL Toronto Maple Leafs 1951 – 55 AHL Boston Bruins 1954 – 66 NHL Detroit Red Wings 1965 – 67 NHL Pittsburgh Penguins 1967 – 69 NHL Minnesota North Stars 1968 – 70 NHL	RS PO	1150 54	72 3	250 10	322 13	1192 59
BOON, DICKIE Belleville, Ontario 1878 – 1961 Inducted 1952	Montreal AAA's 1899 – 03 CAHL Montreal Wanderers 1904 – 06 FAHL	RS* PO*	42 7	10 x	x x	10 x	x x
BOSSY, MIKE Montreal, Quebec 1957 – Inducted 1991	NY Islanders 1977 – 87 NHL	RS PO	752 129	573 85	553 75	1126 160	210 38
BOUCHARD, BUTCH Montreal, Quebec 1920 – Inducted 1966	Montreal Canadiens 1941 – 56 NHL	RS PO	785 113	49 11	144 21	193 32	863 121
BOUCHER, FRANK Ottawa, Ontario 1901 – 1977 Inducted 1958	Ottawa Senators 1921 – 22 NHL Vancouver Maroons 1922 – 24 PCHA Vancouver Maroons 1924 – 26 WCHL NY Rangers 1926 – 38 & 1943 – 44 NHL	RS PO	557 56	161 16	262 18	423 34	119 12
BOUCHER, GEORGE Ottawa, Ontario 1896 – 1960 Inducted 1960	Ottawa Senators 1915 – 17 NHA Ottawa Senators 1917 – 29 NHL Montreal Maroons 1928 – 31 NHL Chicago Blackhawks 1931 – 32 NHL	RS PO	457 44	122 11	62 4	184 15	739 84
BOWIE, RUSSELL "DUBBIE" Montreal, Quebec 1880 – 1959 Inducted 1945	Montreal Victorias 1898 – 05 CAHL Montreal Victorias 1905 – 08 ECAHA	RS* PO*	80 4	234 1	x x	234 1	x x
BROADBENT, HARRY "PUNCH" Ottawa, Ontario 1892 – 1971 Inducted 1962	Ottawa Senators 1912 – 15 NHA Ottawa Sentors 1918 – 24 & 1927 – 28 NHL Montreal Maroons 1924 – 27 NHL NY Americans 1928 – 29 NHL	RS PO	302 41	122 13	45 3	167 16	553 69
BUCYK, JOHN Edmonton, Alberta 1935 – Inducted 1981	Edmonton Flyers 1953 – 56 WHL Detroit Red Wings 1955 – 78 NHL Boston Bruins 1957 – 78 NHL	RS PO	1540 124	556 41	813 62	1369 103	497 42
BURCH, BILLY Yonkers, New York 1900 – 1950 Inducted 1974	Hamilton Tigers 1922 – 25 NHL NY Americans 1925 – 32 NHL Boston/Chicago 1932 – 33 NHL	RS PO	390 2	137 0	53 0	190 0	251 0

			Games Played	Goals	Assists	Total Points	Penalty Minutes
CAMERON, HARRY Pembroke, Ontario 1890 – 1953 Inducted 1962	Toronto Blue Shirts 1912 – 16 NHA Montreal Wanderers 1916 – 17 NHA Toronto Arenas 1917 – 19 NHL Ottawa Senators 1918 – 19 NHL Montreal Canadiens 1919 – 20 NHL Toronto St. Pats 1919 – 23 NHL Saskatoon Crescents 1923 – 25 WCHL Saskatoon Crescents 1925 – 26 WHL	RS† PO†	312 28	174 9	27 1	201 10	154 29
CLANCY, FRANCIS "KING" Ottawa, Ontario 1903 – 1986 Inducted 1958	Ottawa Senators 1921 – 30 NHL Toronto Maple Leafs 1930 – 37 NHL	RS PO	592 61	137 9	143 8	280 17	904 92
CLAPPER, AUBREY "DIT" Newmarket, Ontario 1907 – 1978 Inducted 1947	Boston Bruins 1927 – 47 NHL	RS PO	833 86	228 13	246 17	474 30	462 50
CLARKE, BOBBY Flin Flon, Manitoba 1949 – Inducted 1987	Flin Flon Bombers 1967 – 69 WHL Philadelphia Flyers 1969 – 84 NHL	RS PO	1144 136	358 42	852 77	1210 119	1453 152
CLEGHORN, SPRAGUE Montreal, Quebec 1890 – 1956 Inducted 1958	Ren. Cream. Kings 1910 – 11 NHA Montreal Wanderers 1911 – 17 NHA Ottawa Senators 1918 – 21 NHL Toronto St. Pats 1920 – 21 NHL Montreal Canadiens 1921 – 25 NHL Boston Bruins 1925 – 28 NHL	RS† PO†	377 41	163 6	39 9	202 15	489 48
COLVILLE, NEIL Edmonton, Alberta 1914 – 1987 Inducted 1967	NY Rangers 1935 – 42 & 1944 – 49 NHL Philadelphia Arrows 1935 – 36 CAHL New Haven Ramblers 1948 – 50 AHL	RS PO	464 46	99 7	166 19	265 26	213 33
CONACHER, CHARLIE Toronto, Ontario 1909 – 1967 Inducted 1961	Toronto Maple Leafs 1929 – 38 NHL Detroit Red Wings 1938 – 39 NHL NY Americans 1939 – 41 NHL	RS PO	460 49	225 17	173 18	398 35	523 53
COOK, BILL Brantford, Ontario 1896 – 1986 Inducted 1952	Saskatoon Crescents 1921 – 25 WCHL Saskatoon Crescents 1925 – 26 WHL NY Rangers 1926 – 37 NHL	RS PO	586 50	322 15	196 12	518 27	483 66
COULTER, ART Winnipeg, Manitoba 1909 – Inducted 1974	Chicago Blackhawks 1931 – 36 NHL NY Rangers 1935 – 42 NHL	RS PO	465 49	30 4	82 5	112 9	543 61
COURNOYER, YVAN Drummondville, Quebec 1943 – Inducted 1982	Montreal Canadiens 1963 – 79 NHL Quebec Aces 1964 – 65 AHL	RS PO	968 147	428 64	435 63	863 127	255 47
COWLEY, BILL Bristol, Quebec 1912 – Inducted 1968	St. Louis Eagles 1934 – 35 NHL Boston Bruins 1935 – 47 NHL	RS PO	549 64	195 13	353 33	548 46	143 22
CRAWFORD, RUSTY Cardinal, Ontario 1885 – 1971 Inducted 1962	Quebec Bulldogs 1912 – 17 NHA Toronto Arenas 1917 – 19 NHL Ottawa Senators 1917 – 18 NHL Saskatoon Sheiks 1921 – 23 WCHL Calgary Tigers 1922 – 25 WCHL Vancouver Maroons 1925 – 26 NHL	RS† PO†	245 15	110 6	3 1	113 7	51 0
DARRAGH, JACK Ottawa, Ontario 1890 – 1924 Inducted 1962	Ottawa Senators 1910 – 17 NHA Ottawa Senators 1917 – 24 NHL	RS† PO†	250 30	194 19	21 2	215 21	88 7
DAVIDSON, ALLAN "SCOTTY" Kingston, Ontario 1890 – 1915 Inducted 1950	Toronto Blueshirts 1912 – 14 NHA	RS* PO*	40 4	42 3	x x	42 3	x x

			Games Played	Goals	Assists	Total Points	Penalty Minutes
DAY, CLARENCE "HAPPY" Owen Sound, Ontario 1901 – 1990 Inducted 1961	Toronto St. Pats 1924 – 26 NHL Toronto Maple Leafs 1926 – 37 NHL NY Americans 1937 – 38 NHL	RS PO	581 53	86 4	116 7	202 11	602 56
DELVECCHIO, ALEX Fort William, Ontario 1931 – Inducted 1977	Detroit Red Wings 1950 – 74 NHL Indianapolis Capitols 1951 – 52 AHL	RS PO	1549 121	456 35	825 69	1281 104	383 29
DENNENY, CY Farran's Point, Ontario 1897 – 1970 Inducted 1959	Toronto Shamrocks 1914 – 15 NHA Toronto Arenas 1915 – 16 NHA Ottawa Senators 1916 – 17 NHA Ottawa Senators 1917 – 28 NHL Boston Bruins 1928 – 29 NHL	RS† PO†	368 43	281 19	69 3	350 22	210 31
DIONNE, MARCEL Drummondville, Quebec 1951 – Inducted 1992	Detroit Red Wings 1971 – 75 NHL LA Kings 1975 – 87 NHL NY Rangers 1987 – 89 NHL Denver Rangers 1988 – 89 IHL	RS PO	1348 49	731 21	1040 24	1771 45	600 17
DRILLON, GORDIE Moncton, New Brunswick 1914 – 1986 Inducted 1975	Toronto Maple Leafs 1936 – 42 NHL Montreal Canadiens 1942 – 43 NHL	RS PO	311 50	155 26	139 15	294 41	56 10
DRINKWATER, GRAHAM Montreal, Quebec 1875 – 1946 Inducted 1950	Montreal AAA's 1892 – 93 AHA Montreal Victorias 1893, 1895 – 98 AHA McGill University 1894 – 95 Montreal Victorias 1899 CAHL	RS* PO*	37 4	40 2	x x	40 2	x x
DUMART, WOODY Kitchener, Ontario 1916 – Inducted 1992	Boston Cubs 1935 – 36 CAHL Providence Reds 1936 – 37 IAHL Boston Bruins 1935 – 1942 & 1945 – 54 NHL Providence Reds 1954 – 55 AHL	RS PO	771 88	211 12	218 15	429 27	99 23
DUNDERDALE, TOMMY Benella, Australia 1887 – 1960 Inducted 1974	Winnipeg Victorias 1906 – 08 MHL Toronto Shamrocks 1909 – 10 NHA Quebec Bulldogs 1910 – 11 NHA Victoria Aristocrats 1911 – 15 & 1918 – 23 PCHA Portland Rosebuds 1915 – 18 PCHA Saskatoon/Edmonton 1923 – 24 WCHL	RS* PO*	290 12	225 6	x x	225 6	x x
DUTTON, MERVYN "RED" Russell, Manitoba 1898 – 1987 Inducted 1958	Calgary Tigers 1921 – 26 WCHL Montreal Maroons 1926 – 30 NHL NY Americans 1930 – 36 NHL	RS PO	449 18	29 1	67 0	96 1	871 33
DYE, CECIL "BABE" Hamilton, Ontario 1898 – 1962 Inducted 1970	Toronto St. Pats 1919 – 26 NHL Hamilton Tigers 1920 – 21 NHL Chicago Blackhawks 1926 – 28 NHL NY Americans 1928 – 29 NHL Toronto Maple Leafs 1930 – 31 NHL	RS PO	270 15	202 11	41 2	243 13	190 11
ESPOSITO, PHIL Sault Ste. Marie, Ontario 1942 – Inducted 1984	Sault Ste. Marie Thunderbirds 1961 – 62 EPHL St. Louis Braves 1962 – 64 EPHL Chicago Blackhawks 1963 – 67 NHL Boston Bruins 1967 – 76 NHL NY Rangers 1975 – 81 NHL	RS PO	1282 130	717 61	873 76	1590 137	910 137
FARRELL, ARTHUR ———— 1877 – 1909 Inducted 1965	Montreal Shamrocks 1896 – 97 AHA Montreal Shamrocks 1898 – 01 CAHL	RS* PO*	26 8	29 13	x x	29 13	x x
FLAMAN, FERNIE Dysart, Saskatchewan 1927 – Inducted 1990	Boston Bruins 1944 – 51 & 1954 – 61 NHL Hershey Bears 1946 – 47 AHL Toronto Maple Leafs 1950 – 54 NHL Providence Reds 1961 – 64 AHL	RS PO	910 63	34 4	174 8	208 12	1370 93
FOYSTON, FRANK Minesing, Ontario 1891 – 1966 Inducted 1958	Toronto Blueshirts 1912 – 16 NHA Seattle Metros 1915 – 24 PCHA Victoria Aristocrats 1924 – 26 WCHL Detroit Cougars 1926 – 28 NHL	RS† PO†	357 19	242 14	7 x	249 14	32 x
FREDRICKSON, FRANK Winnipeg, Manitoba 1895 – 1979 Inducted 1958	Victoria Aristocrats 1920 – 24 PCHA Victoria Aristocrats 1924 – 26 WCHL Boston Bruins 1926 – 29 NHL Detroit Falcons 1926 – 27 & 1930 – 31 NHL Pittsburgh Pirates 1928 – 30 NHL	RS† PO†	327 28	170 13	34 5	204 18	206 26

Player	Teams		Games Played	Goals	Assists	Total Points	Penalty Minutes
GADSBY, BILL Calgary, Alberta 1927 – Inducted 1970	Kansas City Play-Mors 1946 – 47 USHL Chicago Blackhawks 1946 – 55 NHL NY Rangers 1954 – 61 NHL Detroit Red Wings 1961 – 66 NHL	RS PO	1248 67	130 4	437 23	567 27	1539 92
GAINEY, BOB Peterborough, Ontario 1953 – Inducted 1992	Nova Scotia Voyageurs 1973 – 74 AHL Montreal Canadiens 1973 – 89 NHL	RS PO	1160 182	239 25	262 48	501 73	585 151
GARDINER, HERB Winnipeg, Manitoba 1891 – 1972 Inducted 1958	Calgary Tigers 1921 – 26 WCHL Montreal Canadiens 1926 – 29 NHL Chicago Blackhawks 1928 – 29 NHL	RS† PO†	233 20	44 3	9 1	53 4	52 10
GARDNER, JIMMY Montreal, Quebec 1881 – 1940 Inducted 1962	Montreal AAA's 1900 – 03 CAHL Montreal Wanderers 1903 – 04 FAHL Montreal Shamrocks 1907 – 08 ECAHA Montreal Wanderers 1908 – 09 ECHA Montreal Wanderers 1909 – 11 NHA New Westminster Royals 1911 – 13 PCHA Montreal Canadiens 1913 – 15 NHA	RS* PO*	112 9	63 2	x x	63 2	x x
GEOFFRION, BERNIE "BOOM BOOM" Montreal, Quebec 1931 – Inducted 1972	Montreal Canadiens 1951 – 64 NHL NY Rangers 1966 – 68 NHL	RS PO	883 132	393 58	429 60	822 118	689 88
GERARD, EDDIE Ottawa, Ontario 1890 – 1937 Inducted 1945	Ottawa Victorias 1907 – 08 FAHL Ottawa Senators 1913 – 17 NHA Ottawa Senators 1917 – 23 NHL Toronto St. Patricks 1921 – 22 NHL	RS† PO†	201 35	93 9	30 1	123 10	106 52
GILBERT, ROD Montreal, Quebec 1941 – Inducted 1982	Trois Rivières Lions 1959 – 60 EPHL Kitchener-Waterloo Beavers 1961 – 62 EPHL NY Rangers 1960 – 78 NHL	RS PO	1065 79	406 34	615 33	1021 67	508 43
GILMOUR, BILLY Ottawa, Ontario 1885 – 1959 Inducted 1962	Ottawa Senators 1902 – 04 CAHL Ottawa Senators 1904 – 05 FAHL Ottawa Senators 1905 – 06 ECAHA Montreal Victorias 1907 – 08 ECAHA Ottawa Senators 1908 – 09 ECHA Ottawa Senators 1915 – 16 NHA	RS* PO*	32 9	26 7	x x	26 7	x x
GOHEEN, FRANK "MOOSE" White Bear, Minnesota 1894 – 1979 Inducted 1952	St. Paul Athletic Club 1914 – 28	RS PO	x x	x x	x x	x x	x x
GOODFELLOW "EBBIE" Ottawa, Ontario 1907 – 1985 Inducted 1963	Detroit Cougars 1928 – 29 CPHL Detroit Cougars 1929 – 30 NHL Detroit Falcons 1930 – 33 NHL Detroit Red Wings 1933 – 43 NHL	RS PO	554 45	134 8	190 8	324 16	511 65
GRANT, MIKE ——— 1874 – 1961 Inducted 1950	Montreal Victorias 1893 – 98 AHA Montreal Victorias 1898 – 1900 & 1901 – 02 CAHL Montreal Shamrocks 1900 – 01 CAHL	RS* PO*	55 8	10 0	x x	10 0	x x
GREEN, WILF "SHORTY" Sudbury, Ontario 1896 – 1960 Inducted 1962	Hamilton Tigers 1923 – 25 NHL NY Americans 1925 – 27 NHL	RS PO	103 0	33 0	8 0	41 0	151 0
GRIFFIS, SI prob. Onaga, Kansas 1883 – 1950 Inducted 1950	Rat Portage Thistles 1902 – 06 MNSHA Kenora Thistles 1906 – 07 MHL Vancouver Millionaires 1911 – 19 PCHA	RS* PO*	117 18	39 5	x x	39 5	x x
HALL, JOE Staffordshire, England 1882 – 1919 Inducted 1961	Winnipeg Victorias 1903 – 05 MHL Quebec Bulldogs 1905 – 06 ECAHA Brandon 1906 – 07 MHL Montreal AAA's 1907 – 08 ECAHA Montreal Shamrocks 1907 – 08 ECAHA Montreal Wanderers 1908 – 09 ECHA Montreal Shamrocks 1909 – 10 NHA Quebec Bulldogs 1910 – 17 NHA Montreal Canadiens 1917 – 19 NHL	RS† PO†	198 22	105 9	1 2	106 11	145 31
HARVEY, DOUG Montreal, Quebec 1924 – 1989 Inducted 1973	Buffalo Bisons 1947 – 48 AHL Montreal Canadiens 1947 – 61 NHL NY Rangers 1961 – 64 NHL St. Paul Rangers 1963 – 64 CPHL Quebec Aces 1963 – 65 AHL Baltimore Clippers 1965 – 67 AHL Pittsburgh Hornets 1966 – 67 AHL Detroit Red Wings 1966 – 67 NHL Kansas City Blues 1967 – 68 CPHL St. Louis Blues 1967 – 69 NHL	RS PO	1113 137	88 8	452 64	540 72	1216 152
HAY, GEORGE Listowel, Ontario 1898 – 1975 Inducted 1958	Regina Capitals 1921 – 25 WCHL Portland Capitals 1925 – 26 WHL Chicago Blackhawks 1926 – 27 NHL Detroit Cougars 1927 – 30 NHL Detroit Falcons 1930 – 31 NHL Detroit Red Wings 1932 – 34 NHL	RS† PO†	373 18	179 5	60 3	239 8	84 2
HEXTALL, BRYAN Grenfell, Saskatchewan 1913 – 1984 Inducted 1969	NY Rangers 1936 – 44 & 1945 – 48 NHL	RS PO	447 37	187 8	175 9	362 17	227 19
HOOPER, TOM Kenora, Ontario 1883 – 1960 Inducted 1962	Rat Portage Thistles 1901 – 05 MNSHA Kenora Thistles 1906 – 07 MHL Montreal Wanderers 1907 – 08 ECAHA Montreal AAA's 1907 – 08 ECAHA	RS* PO*	11 12	12 6	x x	12 6	x x
HORNER, G. REGINALD "RED" Lynden, Ontario 1909 – Inducted 1965	Toronto Maple Leafs 1928 – 40 NHL	RS PO	490 71	42 7	110 10	152 17	1264 160
HORTON, TIM Cochrane, Ontario 1930 – 1974 Inducted 1977	Pittsburgh 1949 – 52 AHL Toronto Maple Leafs 1949 – 70 NHL NY Rangers 1969 – 71 NHL Pittsburgh Penguins 1971 – 72 NHL Buffalo Sabres 1972 – 74 NHL	RS PO	1446 126	115 11	403 39	518 50	1611 183
HOWE, GORDIE Floral, Saskatchewan 1928 – Inducted 1972	Omaha 1945 – 46 USHL Detroit Red Wings 1946 – 71 NHL Houston Aeros 1973 – 77 WHA New England Whalers 1977 – 79 WHA Hartford Whalers 1979 – 80 NHL	RS PO	1767 157	801 68	1049 92	1850 160	1685 220
HOWE, SYD Ottawa, Ontario 1911 – 1976 Inducted 1965	Ottawa Senators 1929 – 30 & 1932 – 34 NHL Philadelphia Quakers 1930 – 31 NHL Toronto Maple Leafs 1931 – 32 NHL St. Louis Eagles 1934 – 35 NHL Detroit Red Wings 1934 – 46 NHL	RS PO	691 70	237 17	291 27	528 44	214 10
HOWELL, HARRY Hamilton, Ontario 1932 – Inducted 1979	Cincinnati Mohawks 1951 – 52 AHL NY Rangers 1952 – 69 NHL Oakland Seals 1969 – 70 NHL California Golden Seals 1970 – 71 NHL LA Kings 1970 – 73 NHL New Jersey Knights 1973 – 74 WHA San Diego Mariners 1974 – 75 WHA Calgary Cowboys 1975 – 76 WHA	RS PO	1411 38	94 3	324 3	418 6	1298 32
HULL, ROBERT (BOBBY) Pointe Anne, Ontario 1939 – Inducted 1983	Chicago Blackhawks 1957 – 72 NHL Winnipeg Jets 1972 – 79 WHA Winnipeg Jets 1979 – 80 NHL Hartford Whalers 1979 – 80 NHL	RS PO	1063 119	610 62	560 67	1170 129	640 102
HYLAND, HARRY Montreal, Quebec 1889 – 1969 Inducted 1962	Montreal Shamrocks 1908 – 09 ECHA Montreal Wanderers 1909 – 11 & 1912 – 17 NHA New Westminster Royals 1911 – 12 PCHA Montreal/Ottawa 1917 – 18 NHL	RS† PO†	157 3	199 3	x x	199 3	9 x
IRVIN, DICK Limestone Ridge, Ontario 1892 – 1957 Inducted 1958	Portland Rosebuds 1916 – 17 PCHA Regina Capitals 1921 – 25 WCHL Portland Capitals 1925 – 26 WHL Chicago Blackhawks 1926 – 29 NHL	RS† PO†	249 12	152 6	23 x	174 6	76 0
JACKSON, HARVEY Toronto, Ontario 1911 – 1966 Inducted 1971	Toronto Maple Leafs 1929 – 39 NHL NY Americans 1939 – 41 NHL Boston Bruins 1941 – 44 NHL	RS PO	636 72	241 18	234 12	475 30	437 55

			Games Played	Goals	Assists	Total Points	Penalty Minutes
JOHNSON, IVAN WILFRED "CHING" Winnipeg, Manitoba 1897 – 1979 Inducted 1958	NY Rangers 1926 – 37 NHL NY Americans 1937 – 38 NHL	RS	435	38	48	86	808
		PO	60	5	2	7	159
JOHNSON, ERNIE Montreal, Quebec 1886 – 1963 Inducted 1952	Montreal Victorias 1903 – 05 CAHL Montreal Wanderers 1905 – 08 ECAHA Montreal Wanderers 1908 – 09 ECHA Montreal Wanderers 1909 – 11 NHA New Westminster Royals 1911 – 14 PCHA Portland Rosebuds 1914 – 18 PCHA Victoria Aristocrats 1918 – 22 PCHA	RS*	270	123	x	123	x
		PO*	21	20	x	123	x
JOHNSON, TOM Baldur, Manitoba 1928 – Inducted 1970	Montreal Canadiens 1947 – 48 & 1949 – 63 NHL Buffalo Bisons 1947 – 50 AHL Boston Bruins 1963 – 65 NHL	RS	978	51	213	264	960
		PO	111	8	15	23	109
JOLIAT, AURÈLE Ottawa, Ontario 1901 – 1986 Inducted 1947	Aberdeen 1916 – 17 OCHL Ottawa New Edinburghs 1917 – 19 —— Iroquois Falls 1919 – 21 —— Montreal Canadiens 1922 – 38 NHL	RS	654	270	190	460	752
		PO	54	14	19	33	89
KEATS, GORDON "DUKE" Montreal, Quebec 1895 – 1972 Inducted 1958	Toronto Blue Shirts 1915 – 17 NHA Edmonton Eskimos 1921 – 25 WCHL Edmonton Eskimos 1925 – 26 WHL Boston & Detroit 1926 – 27 NHL Detroit & Chicago 1927 – 28 NHL Chicago Blackhawks 1928 – 29 NHL	RS†	256	183	19	202	112
		PO†	8	2	x	2	x
KELLY, LEONARD "RED" Simcoe, Ontario 1927 – Inducted 1969	Detroit Red Wings 1947 – 60 NHL Toronto Maple Leafs 1959 – 67 NHL	RS	1316	281	542	823	327
		PO	164	33	59	92	51
KENNEDY, TED "TEEDER" Humberstone, Ontario 1925 – Inducted 1966	Toronto Maple Leafs 1942 – 55 & 1956 – 57 NHL	RS	696	231	329	560	432
		PO	78	29	31	60	32
KEON, DAVE Noranda, Quebec 1940 – Inducted 1986	Sudbury Wolves 1959 – 60 EPHL Toronto Maple Leafs 1960 – 75 NHL Indianapolis Racers 1975 – 76 WHA Minneapolis Saints 1975 – 77 WHA New England Whalers 1976 – 79 WHA Hartford Whalers 1979 – 82 NHL	RS	1296	396	590	986	117
		PO	92	32	36	68	6
LACH, ELMER Nokomis, Saskatchewan 1918 – Inducted 1966	Montreal Canadiens 1940 – 54 NHL	RS	664	215	408	623	478
		PO	76	19	45	64	36
LAFLEUR, GUY Thurso, Quebec 1951 – Inducted 1988	Montreal Canadiens 1971 – 85 NHL NY Rangers 1988 – 89 NHL Quebec Nordiques 1989 – 91 NHL	RS	1126	560	793	1353	399
		PO	128	58	76	134	67
LALONDE, EDOUARD "NEWSY" Cornwall, Ontario 1887 – 1971 Inducted 1950	Cornwall 1904 – 05 FAHL Portage Lakers 1907 – 08 MHL Toronto Maple Leafs 1907 – 09 OPHL Montreal & Renfrew 1909 – 10 NHA Montreal Canadiens 1910 – 11 & 1912 – 17 NHA Vancouver Millionaires 1911 – 12 PCHA Montreal Canadiens 1917 – 22 NHL Saskatoon Crescents 1922 – 25 WCHL Saskatoon Crescents 1925 – 26 WHL NY Americans 1926 – 27 NHL	RS†	315	428	27	455	122
		PO†	29	27	1	28	19
LAPERRIERE, JACQUES Rouyn, Quebec 1941 – Inducted 1987	Ottawa – Hull Canadiens 1959 – 63 EPHL Montreal Canadiens 1962 – 74 NHL	RS	691	40	242	282	674
		PO	88	9	22	31	101
LAVIOLETTE, JACK Belleville, Ontario 1879 – 1960 Inducted 1962	Montreal Nationals 1903 – 04 FAHL —— 1904 – 07 IPL Montreal Shamrocks 1907 – 08 ECAHA Montreal Shamrocks 1908 – 09 ECHA Montreal Canadiens 1909 – 17 NHA Montreal Canadiens 1917 – 18 NHL	RS†	178	58	0	58	0
		PO†	14	1	0	1	0
LEMAIRE, JACQUES LaSalle, Quebec 1945 – Inducted 1984	Quebec Aces 1964 – 65 AHL Houston Apollos 1966 – 67 CPHL Montreal Canadiens 1967 – 79 NHL	RS	853	366	469	835	217
		PO	145	61	78	139	63
LEWIS, HERBIE Calgary, Alberta 1907 – Inducted 1989	Detroit Cougars 1928 – 30 NHL Detroit Falcons 1930 – 33 NHL Detroit Red Wings 1933 – 39 NHL	RS	484	148	161	309	248
		PO	38	13	10	23	6
LINDSAY, TED Renfrew, Ontario 1925 – Inducted 1966	Detroit Red Wings 1944 – 57 & 1964 – 65 NHL Chicago Blackhawks 1957 – 60 NHL	RS	1068	379	472	851	1808
		PO	133	47	49	96	194
MACKAY, MICKEY Chesley, Ontario 1894 – 1940 Inducted 1952	Vancouver Millionaires 1914 – 19 & 1920 – 24 PCHA Vancouver Maroons 1924 – 25 WCHL Vancouver Maroons 1925 – 26 WHL Chicago Blackhawks 1926 – 28 NHL Boston & Pittsburgh 1928 – 29 NHL Boston Bruins 1929 – 30 NHL	RS†	388	246	19	265	79
		PO†	50	19	0	19	6
MAHOVLICH, FRANK Timmins, Ontario 1938 – Inducted 1981	Toronto Maple Leafs 1956 – 68 NHL Detroit Red Wings 1967 – 71 NHL Montreal Canadiens 1970 – 74 NHL Toronto Toros 1974 – 76 WHA Birmingham Bulls 1976 – 78 WHA	RS	1181	533	570	1103	1056
		PO	137	51	67	118	163
MALONE, "PHANTOM" JOE Sillery, Quebec 1890 – 1969 Inducted 1950	Quebec Bulldogs 1908 – 09 ECHA Waterloo 1909 – 10 OPHL Quebec Bulldogs 1910 – 17 NHA Montreal Canadiens 1917 – 19 & 1920 – 21 & 1922 – 24 NHL Quebec Bulldogs 1919 – 20 NHL Hamilton Tigers 1921 – 22 NHL	RS	125	146	18	164	35
		PO	7	7	1	8	0
MANTHA, SYLVIO Montreal, Quebec 1902 – 1974 Inducted 1960	Montreal Canadiens 1923 – 36 NHL Boston Bruins 1936 – 37 NHL	RS	543	63	72	135	667
		PO	46	5	4	9	66
MARSHALL, JACK St. Vallier, Quebec 1877 – 1965 Inducted 1965	Winnipeg Victorias 1900 – 01 MHL Montreal Victorias 1901 – 03 CAHL Montreal Wanderers 1903 – 05 FAHL Montreal Montagnards 1905 – 06 FAHL Montreal Wanderers 1906 – 07 ECAHA Montreal Shamrocks 1907 – 08 ECAHA Montreal Shamrocks 1908 – 09 ECHA Montreal Wanderers 1909 – 12 NHA Toronto Tecumsehs 1912 – 13 NHA Toronto Ontarios 1913 – 14 NHA Toronto Shamrocks 1914 – 15 NHA Montreal Wanderers 1915 – 17 NHA	RS*	132	99	x	99	x
		PO*	18	13	x	13	x
MAXWELL, FRED Winnipeg, Manitoba 1890 – 1975 Inducted 1962	Winnipeg Monarchs 1914 – 16 MSHL Winnipeg Falcons 1918 – 25 MSHL	RS	x	x	x	x	x
		PO	x	x	x	x	x
McDONALD, LANNY Hanna, Alberta 1953 – Inducted 1992	Medicine Hat Tigers 1971 – 73 WHL Toronto Maple Leafs 1973 – 80 NHL Colorado Rockies 1979 – 82 NHL Calgary Flames 1981 – 89 NHL	RS	1111	500	506	1006	899
		PO	117	44	40	84	120
McGEE, FRANK Ottawa, Ontario Born late 1800's – 1916 Inducted 1945	Ottawa Senators 1902 – 04 CAHL Ottawa Senators 1904 – 05 FAHL Ottawa Senators 1905 – 06 ECAHA	RS*	23	71	x	71	x
		PO*	22	63	x	63	x
McGIMSIE, BILLY Woodsville, Ontario 1880 – 1968 Inducted 1962	Rat Portage Thistles 1902 – 03 & 1904 – 06 MHSHA Kenora Thistles 1906 – 07 MHL	RS*	x	x	x	x	x
		PO*	7	4	x	4	x
McNAMARA, GEORGE Penetang, Ontario 1886 – 1952 Inducted 1958	Montreal Shamrocks 1907 – 08 ECAHA Montreal Shamrocks 1908 – 09 ECHA Halifax Crescents 1909 – 12 MPL Waterloo 1911 OPHL Toronto Tecumsehs 1912 – 13 NHA Ottawa/Ontario 1913 – 14 NHA Toronto Shamrocks 1914 – 15 NHA Toronto Blueshirts 1915 – 16 NHA 228th Battalion 1916 – 17 NHA	RS*	121	39	x	39	x
		PO*	3	2	x	2	x

Player	Teams		Games Played	Goals	Assists	Total Points	Penalty Minutes
MIKITA, STAN Skolce, Czechoslovakia 1940 – Inducted 1983	Chicago Blackhawks 1958 – 80 NHL	RS	1394	541	926	1467	1270
		PO	155	59	91	150	169
MOORE, DICKIE Montreal, Quebec 1931 – Inducted 1974	Montreal Royals 1951 – 52 QSHL Montreal Canadiens 1951 – 63 NHL Buffalo Bisons 1952 – 53 AHL Montreal Royals 1953 – 54 QHL Toronto Maple Leafs 1964 – 65 NHL St. Louis Blues 1967 – 68 NHL	RS	719	261	347	608	652
		PO	135	46	64	110	122
MORENZ, HOWIE Mitchell, Ontario 1902 – 1937 Inducted 1945	Montreal Canadiens 1923 – 34 & 1936 – 37 NHL Chicago Blackhawks 1934 – 36 NHL NY Rangers 1935 – 36 NHL	RS	550	270	197	467	531
		PO	47	21	11	32	68
MOSIENKO, BILL Winnipeg, Manitoba 1921 – Inducted 1965	Providence Reds 1940 – 41 AHL Kansas City Greyhounds 1940 – 42 AHA Chicago Blackhawks 1941 – 55 NHL Winnipeg Warriors 1955 – 59 WHL	RS	711	258	282	540	121
		PO	22	10	4	14	15
NIGHBOR, FRANK Pembroke, Ontario 1893 – 1966 Inducted 1947	Toronto Blueshirts 1912 – 13 NHA Vancouver Millionaires 1913 – 15 PCHA Ottawa Senators 1915 – 17 NHA Ottawa Senators 1917 – 29 NHL Toronto Maple Leafs 1929 – 30 NHL	RS	348	136	60	196	266
		PO	36	11	10	21	27
NOBLE, REGINALD (REG) Collingwood, Ontario 1895 – 1962 Inducted 1962	Canadiens/Toronto 1916 – 17 NHA Toronto Arenas 1917 – 19 NHL Toronto St. Patricks 1919 – 25 NHL Montreal Maroons 1924 – 27 NHL Detroit Cougars 1927 – 32 NHL Detroit & Montreal 1932 – 33 NHL	RS†	534	180	79	259	770
		PO†	34	4	5	9	39
O'CONNOR, BUDDY Montreal, Quebec 1916 – 1977 Inducted 1988	Montreal Canadiens 1941 – 47 NHL NY Rangers 1947 – 51 NHL Cincinnati Mohawks 1951 – 52 AHL	RS	509	140	257	397	34
		PO	53	15	21	36	6
OLIVER, HARRY Selkirk, Manitoba 1898 – 1985 Inducted 1967	Calgary Tigers 1921 – 25 WCHL Calgary Tigers 1925 – 26 WHL Boston Bruins 1926 – 34 NHL NY Americans 1934 – 37 NHL	RS†	603	216	85	301	147
		PO†	47	13	6	19	22
OLMSTEAD, BERT Scepter, Saskatchewan 1926 – Inducted 1985	Kansas City Play-Mors 1946 – 49 USHL Chicago Blackhawks 1948 – 51 NHL Milwaukee Seagulls 1950 – 51 USHL Montreal Canadiens 1950 – 58 NHL Toronto Maple Leafs 1958 – 62 NHL	RS	848	181	421	602	884
		PO	115	16	42	58	101
ORR, ROBERT (BOBBY) Parry Sound, Ontario 1948 – Inducted 1979	Boston Bruins 1966 – 76 NHL Chicago Blackhawks 1976 – 79 NHL	RS	657	270	645	915	953
		PO	74	26	66	92	107
PARK, BRAD Toronto, Ontario 1948 – Inducted 1988	Buffalo Bisons 1968 – 69 AHL NY Rangers 1968 – 76 NHL Boston Bruins 1975 – 83 NHL Detroit Red Wings 1983 – 85 NHL	RS	1113	213	683	896	1429
		PO	161	35	90	125	217
PATRICK, LESTER Drummondville, Quebec 1883 – 1960 Inducted 1947	Brandon 1903 – 04 MHL Westmount 1904 – 05 CAHL Montreal Wanderers 1905 – 07 ECAHA Edmonton 1907 – 08 ——— Ren. Cream. Kings 1909 – 10 NHA Victoria Aristocrats 1911 – 16 & 1918 – 22 PCHA Spokane Canaries 1916 – 17 PCHA Seattle Metros 1917 – 18 PCHA Victoria Cougars 1925 – 26 WHL NY Rangers 1927 – 28 NHL	RS*	207	130	x	130	x
		PO*	21	20	x	20	x
PATRICK, JOSEPH LYNN Victoria, British Columbia 1912 – 1980 Inducted 1980	NY Rangers 1934 – 43 & 1945 – 46 NHL Newhaven Ramblers 1946 – 47 AHL	RS	455	145	190	335	270
		PO	44	10	6	16	22
PERREAULT, GILBERT Victoriaville, Quebec 1950 – Inducted 1990	Buffalo Sabres 1970 – 87 NHL	RS	1191	512	814	1326	500
		PO	90	33	70	103	44
PHILLIPS, TOM Kenora, Ontario 1880 – 1923 Inducted 1945	Montreal AAA's 1902 – 03 CAHL Toronto Marlboroughs 1903 – 04 OHA Rat Portage Thistles 1904 – 06 MNSHA Kenora Thistles 1906 – 07 MHL Ottawa Senators 1907 – 08 ECAHA Vancouver Millionaires 1911 – 12 PCHA	RS*	33	57	x	57	x
		PO*	16	27	x	27	x
PILOTE, PIERRE Kenogami, Quebec 1931 – Inducted 1975	Buffalo Bisons 1951 – 56 AHL Chicago Blackhawks 1955 – 68 NHL Toronto Maple Leafs 1968 – 69 NHL	RS	890	80	418	498	1251
		PO	86	8	53	61	102
PITRE, DIDIER "CANNONBALL" Valleyfield, Quebec 1883 – 1934 Inducted 1962	Montreal Nationals 1903 – 04 FAHL Montreal Nationals 1904 – 05 CAHL Montreal Shamrocks 1907 – 08 ECAHA Edmonton 1907 – 08 ——— Renfrew Millionaires 1908 – 09 ——— Montreal Canadiens 1909 – 13 & 1914 – 17 NHA Vancouver Millionaires 1913 – 14 PCHA Montreal Canadiens 1917 – 23 NHL	RS†	282	238	17	255	59
		PO†	27	13	2	15	0
POTVIN, DENIS Ottawa, Ontario 1953 – Inducted 1991	NY Islanders 1973 – 88 NHL	RS	1060	310	742	1052	1354
		PO	185	56	108	164	253
PRATT, WALTER "BABE" Stony Mountain, Manitoba 1916 – 1988 Inducted 1966	NY Rangers 1935 – 43 NHL Toronto Maple Leafs 1942 – 46 NHL Boston Bruins 1946 – 47 NHL	RS	517	83	209	292	453
		PO	63	12	17	29	90
PRIMEAU, JOE Lindsay, Ontario 1906 – 1989 Inducted 1963	Toronto 1927 – 28 CPHL London Tecumsehs 1928 – 29 CPHL Toronto Maple Leafs 1927 – 36 NHL	RS	310	66	177	243	105
		PO	38	5	18	23	12
PRONOVOST, MARCEL Lac la Tortue, Quebec 1930 – Inducted 1978	Omaha Knights 1949 – 50 USHL Indianapolis Capitols 1950 – 51 AHL Detroit Red Wings 1949 – 65 NHL Toronto Maple Leafs 1965 – 70 NHL Tulsa 1969 – 71 CHL	RS	1206	88	257	345	851
		PO	134	8	23	31	104
PULFORD, BOB Newton Robinson, Ontario 1936 – Inducted 1991	Toronto Maple Leafs 1956 – 70 NHL LA Kings 1970 – 72 NHL	RS	1079	281	362	643	792
		PO	89	25	26	51	126
PULFORD, HARVEY Toronto, Ontario 1875 – 1940 Inducted 1945	Ottawa Senators 1893 – 98 AHA Ottawa Senators 1900 – 04 CAHL Ottawa Senators 1904 – 05 FAHL Ottawa Senators 1905 – 08 ECAHA	RS*	96	6	x	6	x
		PO*	22	2	x	2	x
QUACKENBUSH, BILL Toronto, Ontario 1922 – Inducted 1976	Indianapolis Capitols 1942 – 44 AHL Detroit Red Wings 1942 – 49 NHL Boston Bruins 1949 – 56 NHL	RS	774	62	222	284	95
		PO	79	2	19	21	8
RANKIN, FRANK Stratford, Ontario 1890 – 1932 Inducted 1961	Stratford 1906 – 09 OHA Eaton's Athletic Association OHA 1910 – 12 OHA St. Michaels 1912 – 14 OHA	RS	x	x	x	x	x
		PO	x	x	x	x	x
RATELLE, JEAN Lac St. Jean, Quebec 1940 – Inducted 1985	Trois Rivières Lions 1959 – 60 EPHL Kitchener-Waterloo Beavers 1961 – 62 EPHL NY Rangers 1962 – 76 NHL Baltimore 1962 – 65 AHL Boston Bruins 1975 – 81 NHL	RS	1281	491	776	1267	276
		PO	123	32	66	98	24
REARDON, KENNETH JOSEPH Winnipeg, Manitoba 1921 – Inducted 1966	Montreal Canadiens 1940 – 42 NHL Ottawa Commandos 1942 – 43 ——— Montreal Canadiens 1945 – 50 NHL	RS	341	26	96	122	604
		PO	31	2	5	7	62
RICHARD, HENRI Montreal, Quebec 1936 – Inducted 1979	Montreal Canadiens 1955 – 75 NHL	RS	1256	358	688	1046	928
		PO	180	49	80	129	181
RICHARD, MAURICE "ROCKET" Montreal, Quebec 1921 – Inducted 1961	Montreal Canadiens 1942 – 60 NHL	RS	978	544	421	965	1285
		PO	133	82	44	126	188

			Games Played	Goals	Assists	Total Points	Penalty Minutes
RICHARDSON, GEORGE Kingston, Ontario 1887 – 1916 Inducted 1950	14th Regiment 1906 – 1912 Queens University 1908 – 09	RS	x	x	x	x	x
		PO	x	x	x	x	x
ROBERTS, GORDON Ottawa, Ontario 1891 – 1966 Inducted 1971	Ottawa Senators 1909 – 10 NHA Montreal Wanderers 1910 – 16 NHA Vancouver Millionaires 1916 – 17 & 1919 – 20 PCHA Seattle Metropolitans 1917 – 18 PCHA	RS*	166	203	x	x	x
		PO*	7	8	x	x	x
ROSS, ART Naughton, Ontario 1886 – 1964 Inducted 1945	Westmount 1904 – 05 CAHL Brandon 1906 – 07 MHL Kenora Thistles 1906 – 07 MHL Montreal Wanderers 1907 – 08 ECAHA Montreal Wanderers 1908 – 09 ECHA Haileybury Comets 1909 – 10 NHA Montreal Wanderers 1910 – 14 & 1916 – 17 NHA Ottawa Senators 1914 – 16 NHA Montreal Wanderers 1917 – 18 NHL	RS†	167	85	0	85	0
		PO†	16	6	0	6	0
RUSSEL, BLAIR Montreal, Quebec 1880 – 1961 Inducted 1965	Montreal Victorias 1899 – 05 CAHL Montreal Victorias 1905 – 08 ECAHA	RS*	67	110	x	110	x
		PO*	2	0	x	0	x
RUSSELL, ERNIE Montreal, Quebec 1883 – 1963 Inducted 1965	Montreal AAA's 1904 – 05 CAHL Montreal Wanderers 1905 – 07 ECAHA Montreal Wanderers 1907 – 08 & 1909 – 14 NHA	RS*	98	180	x	180	x
		PO*	11	31	x	31	x
RUTTAN, JACK Winnipeg, Manitoba 1889 – 1973 Inducted 1962	Armstrong's Point 1905 – 06 Rustler 1906 – 07 St. Johns College 1907 – 08 Manitoba Varsity 1909 – 12 WSHL Winnipeg 1912 – 13 WpgHL	RS	x	x	x	x	x
		PO	x	x	x	x	x
SAVARD, SERGE Montreal, Quebec 1946 – Inducted 1986	Omaha Knights 1964 – 65 CPHL Quebec Aces 1966 – 67 AHL Houston Apollos 1966 – 67 CPHL Montreal Canadiens 1966 – 81 NHL Winnipeg Jets 1981 – 83 NHL	RS	1040	106	333	439	592
		PO	130	19	49	68	88
SCANLAN, FRED ——— ——— Inducted 1965	Montreal Shamrocks 1897 – 98 AHA Montreal Shamrocks 1898 – 01 CAHL Winnipeg Victorias 1901 – 03 MHL	RS*	31	16	x	16	x
		PO*	17	6	x	6	x
SCHMIDT, MILT Kitchener, Ontario 1918 – Inducted 1961	Providence Reds 1936 – 37 IAHL Boston Bruins 1936 – 42 & 1945 – 55 NHL	RS	778	229	346	575	466
		PO	86	24	25	49	60
SCHRINER, SWEENEY Calgary, Alberta 1911 – 1990 Inducted 1962	NY Americans 1934 – 39 NHL Toronto Maple Leafs 1939 – 43 & 1944 – 46 NHL	RS	484	201	204	405	148
		PO	60	18	11	29	44
SEIBERT, EARL Kitchener, Ontario 1911 – 1990 Inducted 1963	NY Rangers 1931 – 36 NHL Chicago Blackhawks 1935 – 45 NHL Detroit Red Wings 1944 – 46 NHL	RS	650	89	187	276	768
		PO	66	11	8	19	76
SEIBERT, OLIVER Berlin, Ontario 1881 – 1944 Inducted 1961	Berlin Dutchmen 1900 – 06 Houghton ——— IHL Guelph ——— OPHL London ——— OPHL	RS	x	x	x	x	x
		PO	x	x	x	x	x
SHORE, EDDIE Fort Qu'Appelle, Saskatchewan 1902 – 1985 Inducted 1947	Regina Capitals 1924 – 25 WCHL Edmonton Eskimo 1925 – 26 WHL Boston Bruins 1926 – 40 NHL	RS	550	105	179	284	1037
		PO	55	6	13	19	179
SIEBERT, ALBERT CHARLES "BABE" Plattsville, Ontario 1904 – 1939 Inducted 1964	Montreal Maroons 1925 – 32 NHL NY Rangers 1932 – 34 NHL Boston Bruins 1933 – 36 NHL Montreal Canadiens 1936 – 39 NHL	RS	593	140	156	296	972
		PO	54	8	7	15	62
SIMPSON, JOE Selkirk, Manitoba 1893 – 1973 Inducted 1962	Edmonton Eskimos 1921 – 25 WCHL NY Americans 1925 – 31 NHL	RS†	340	76	19	95	176
		PO†	8	1	x	1	x
SITTLER, DARRYL St. Jacobs, Ontario 1950 – Inducted 1989	Toronto Maple Leafs 1970 – 82 NHL Philadelphia Flyers 1981 – 84 NHL Detroit Red Wings 1984 – 85 NHL	RS	1096	484	637	1121	948
		PO	76	29	45	74	137
SMITH, ALF Ottawa, Ontario 1873 – 1953 Inducted 1962	Ottawa Senators 1894 – 97 AHA Ottawa Senators 1903 – 04 CAHL Ottawa Senators 1904 – 05 FAHL Ottawa Senators 1905 – 08 ECAHA Kenora Thistles 1906 – 07 MHL	RS*	65	90	x	90	x
		PO*	22	36	x	36	x
SMITH, CLINT Assiniboia, Saskatchewan 1913 – Inducted 1991	NY Rangers 1936 – 43 NHL Chicago Blackhawks 1943 – 47 NHL	RS	483	161	236	397	24
		PO	44	10	14	24	2
SMITH, REGINALD JOSEPH "HOOLEY" Toronto, Ontario 1905 – 1963 Inducted 1972	Ottawa Senators 1924 – 27 NHL Montreal Maroons 1927 – 36 NHL Boston Bruins 1936 – 37 NHL NY Americans 1937 – 41 NHL	RS	715	200	215	415	1013
		PO	54	11	8	19	109
SMITH, TOMMY Ottawa, Ontario 1885 – 1966 Inducted 1973	Ottawa Victorias 1905 – 06 FAHL Ottawa Senators 1905 – 06 ECAHA Brantford Indians 1908 – 10 OPHL Cobalt Silver Kings 1909 – 10 NHA Galt 1910 – 11 OPHL Moncton 1911 – 12 ——— Quebec Bulldogs 1912 – 16 NHA Ontarios 1914 – 15 NHA Montreal Canadiens 1916 – 17 NHA Quebec Bulldogs 1919 – 1920 NHL	RS*	x	240	x	240	x
		PO*	15	15	x	15	x
STANLEY, ALLAN Timmins, Ontario 1926 – Inducted 1981	Providence Reds 1946 – 49 AHL NY Rangers 1948 – 55 NHL Vancouver Canucks 1953 – 54 WHL Chicago Blackhawks 1954 – 56 NHL Boston Bruins 1956 – 58 NHL Toronto Maple Leafs 1958 – 68 NHL Philadelphia Flyers 1968 – 69 NHL	RS	1244	100	333	433	792
		PO	109	7	36	43	80
STANLEY, BARNEY Paisley, Ontario 1893 – 1971 Inducted 1962	Vancouver Millionaires 1914 – 1919 PCHA Calgary Tigers 1921 – 22 WCHL Regina Capitals 1922 – 24 WCHL Edmonton Eskimos 1924 – 25 WCHL Edmonton Eskimos 1925 – 26 WHL	RS*	216	144	x	144	x
		PO*	19	11	x	11	x
STEWART, JACK Pilot Mound, Manitoba 1917 – 1983 Inducted 1964	Pittsburgh Hornets 1937 – 39 IAHL Detroit Red Wings 1938 – 43 & 1945 – 50 NHL Chicago Blackhawks 1950 – 52 NHL	RS	565	31	84	115	765
		PO	80	5	14	19	143
STEWART, NELSON Montreal, Quebec 1902 – 1957 Inducted 1962	Montreal Maroons 1925 – 32 NHL Boston Bruins 1932 – 35 & 1936 – 37 NHL NY Americans 1935 – 40 NHL	RS	651	324	191	515	943
		PO	54	15	13	28	61
STUART, BRUCE Ottawa, Ontario 1882 – 1961 Inducted 1961	Ottawa Senators 1898 – 1900 & 1901 – 02 CAHL Quebec Bulldogs 1900 – 01 CAHL Montreal Wanderers 1907 – 08 ECAHA Ottawa Senators 1908 – 09 ECHA Ottawa Senators 1909 – 11 NHA	RS*	45	63	x	63	x
		PO*	7	17	x	17	x
STUART, WILLIAM HODGSON "HOD" Ottawa, Ontario 1879 – 1907 Inducted 1945	Ottawa Senators 1898 – 1900 CAHL Quebec Bulldogs 1900 – 02 CAHL ——— 1902 – 06 IPL Montreal Wanderers 1906 – 08 ECAHA	RS*	33	16	x	16	x
		PO*	4	0	x	0	x
TAYLOR, FREDERICK "CYCLONE" Tara, Ontario 1883 – 1979 Inducted 1947	Ottawa Senators 1907 – 09 ECAHA Ren. Cream. Kings 1909 – 11 NHA Vancouver Millionaires 1912 – 21 & 1922 – 23 PCHA	RS*	186	194	x	194	x
		PO*	19	15	x	15	x
TRIHEY, HARRY Montreal, Quebec 1877 – 1942 Inducted 1950	Montreal Shamrocks 1896 – 98 AHC Montreal Shamrocks 1898 – 01 CAHL	RS*	30	46	x	46	x
		PO*	8	16	x	16	x

Skaters

Player	Teams		Games Played	Goals	Assists	Total Points	Penalty Minutes
ULLMAN, NORM Provost, Alberta 1935 – Inducted 1982	Edmonton 1953 – 55 WHL Detroit Red Wings 1955 – 68 NHL Toronto Maple Leafs 1967 – 75 NHL Edmonton Oilers 1975 – 77 WHA	RS PO	1410 106	490 30	739 53	1229 83	712 67
WALKER, JACK Silver Mountain, Ontario 1888 – 1950 Inducted 1960	Port Arthur 1910 – 11 —— Toronto Blueshirts 1912 – 15 NHA Seattle Metros 1915 – 24 PCHA Victoria Cougars 1924 – 25 WCHL Victoria Cougars 1925 – 26 WHL Detroit Cougars 1926 – 28 NHL	RS† PO†	361 46	135 20	8 x	143 20	18 x
WALSH, MARTY Kingston, Ontario 1883 – 1915 Inducted 1962	Ottawa Senators 1907 – 08 ECAHA Ottawa Senators 1908 – 09 ECHA Ottawa Senators 1909 – 12 NHA	RS* PO*	59 8	135 25	x x	135 25	x x
WATSON, HARRY "MOOSE" St John's, Newfoundland 1898 – 1957 Inducted 1962	St. Andrews 1915 OHA Aura Lee Juniors 1918 OHA Toronto Dentals 1919 OHA Toronto Granites 1920 – 25 OHL Toronto Sea Fleas 1931 OHA	RS PO	x x	x x	x x	x x	x x
WEILAND, RALPH C. "COONEY" Seaforth, Ontario 1904 – 1985 Inducted 1971	Boston Bruins 1928 – 32 & 1935 – 39 NHL Ottawa Senators 1932 – 34 NHL Detroit Red Wings 1933 – 35 NHL	RS PO	509 45	173 12	160 10	333 22	147 12
WESTWICK, HARRY Ottawa, Ontario 1876 – 1957 Inducted 1962	Ottawa Senators 1894 – 98 AHA Ottawa Senators 1900 – 04 CAHL Ottawa Senators 1904 – 05 FAHL Ottawa Senators 1905 – 08 ECAHA Kenora Thistles 1906 – 07 MHL	RS* PO*	87 24	87 26	x x	87 26	x x
WHITCROFT, FRED Port Perry, Ontario 1882 – 1931 Inducted 1962	Kenora Thistles 1906 – 08 MHL Edmonton 1908 – 10 —— Ren. Cream. Kings 1909 – 10 NHA	RS* PO*	9 8	55 14	x x	5 14	x x
WILSON, GORDON ALLAN "PHAT" Port Arthur, Ontario 1895 – 1970 Inducted 1962	Port Arthur War Veterans 1918 – 20 OHA Iroquois Falls Eskimos 1921 NOHA Port Arthur Bearcats 1923 – 33 OHA	RS PO	x x	x x	x x	x x	x x

Goalies

Player	Teams		Games Played	Minutes	Goals Against	Shutouts	Average
BENEDICT, CLINT Ottawa, Ontario 1891 – 1976 Inducted 1965	Ottawa Senators 1912 – 17 NHA Ottawa Senators 1917 – 24 NHL Montreal Maroons 1924 – 30 NHL	RS PO	362 48	22321 2907	863 87	57 15	2.32 1.80
BOWER, JOHNNY Prince Albert, Saskatchewan 1924 – Inducted 1976	Cleveland Barons 1945 – 53 & 1957 – 58 AHL NY Rangers 1953 – 55 & 56 – 57 NHL Toronto Maple Leafs 1958 – 70 NHL Providence Reds 1945 – 46 & 1955 – 57 AHL Vancouver Canucks 1954 – 55 WHL	RS PO	552 74	32077 4350	1347 184	37 5	2.52 2.54
BRIMSEK, FRANK Eveleth, Minnesota 1915 – Inducted 1966	Boston Bruins 1938 – 43 & 1945 – 49 NHL Chicago Blackhawks 1949 – 50 NHL	RS PO	514 68	31210 4365	1404 186	40 2	2.70 2.56
BRODA, WALTER "TURK" Brandon, Manitoba 1914 – 1972 Inducted 1967	Detroit Olympics 1935 – 36 IHL Toronto Maple Leafs 1936 – 43 & 1945 – 52 NHL	RS PO	629 102	38167 6406	1609 211	62 13	2.53 1.98
CHEEVERS, GERRY St. Catharines, Ontario 1940 – Inducted 1985	Toronto Maple Leafs 1961 – 62 NHL Sault Ste. Marie Thunderbirds 1961 – 62 CPHL Pittsburgh Hornets 1961 – 62 AHL Rochester Americans 1961 – 65 AHL Sudbury Wolves 1962 – 63 EPHL Boston Bruins 1965 – 72 & 1975 – 80 NHL Oklahoma City Blazers 965 – 67 CPHL Cleveland Crusaders 1972 – 76 WHA	RS PO	418 88	24394 5396	1175 242	26 8	2.89 2.69
CONNELL, ALEX Ottawa, Ontario 1902 – 1958 Inducted 1958	Ottawa Senators 1924 – 31 & 1932 – 33 NHL Detroit Falcons 1931 – 32 NHL NY Americans 1933 – 34 NHL Montreal Maroons 1934 – 35 & 1936 – 37 NHL	RS PO	417 21	26030 1309	830 26	81 4	1.91 1.19
DRYDEN, KEN Hamilton, Ontario 1947 – Inducted 1983	Montreal Voyagers 1970 – 71 AHL Montreal Canadiens 1970 – 73 & 1974 – 79 NHL	RS PO	397 112	23352 6846	870 274	46 10	2.24 2.40
DURNAN, BILL Toronto, Ontario 1916 – 1972 Inducted 1964	Montreal Canadiens 1943 – 50 NHL.	RS PO	383 45	22945 2851	901 99	34 2	2.36 2.08
ESPOSITO, TONY Sault Ste. Marie, Ontario 1943 – Inducted 1988	Vancouver Canucks 1967 – 68 WHL Montreal Canadiens 1968 – 69 NHL Houston Apollos 1968 – 69 CHL Chicago Blackhawks 1969 – 84 NHL	RS PO	886 99	52585 6017	2563 308	76 6	2.92 3.07
GARDINER, CHUCK Edinburgh, Scotland 1904 – 1934 Inducted 1945	Chicago Blackhawks 1927 – 34 NHL	RS PO	316 21	19687 1532	664 35	42 5	2.05 1.37
GIACOMIN, EDDIE Sudbury, Ontario 1939 – Inducted 1987	Providence Reds 1959 – 65 AHL Baltimore Clippers 1965 – 66 AHL NY Rangers 1965 – 76 NHL Detroit Red Wings 1975 – 78 NHL	RS PO	610 65	35693 3834	1675 180	54 1	2.82 2.82
HAINSWORTH, GEORGE Toronto, Ontario 1895 – 1950 Inducted 1961	Saskatoon Crescents 1923 – 25 WCHL Saskatoon Crescents 1925 – 26 WHL Montreal Canadiens 1926 – 33 & 1936 – 37 NHL Toronto Maple Leafs 1933 – 37 NHL	RS PO	465 52	29415 3486	937 112	94 8	1.91 1.93
HALL, GLENN Humboldt, Saskatchewan 1931 – Inducted 1975	Indianapolis Capitols 1951 – 52 AHL Detroit Red Wings 1952 – 53 & 1954 – 57 NHL Edmonton Flyers 1952 – 55 WHL Chicago Blackhawks 1957 – 67 NHL St. Louis Blues 1967 – 71 NHL	RS PO	906 115	53464 6899	2239 321	84 6	2.51 2.79
HERN, RILEY St. Mary's, Ontario 1880 – 1929 Inducted 1962	Montreal Wanderers 1906 – 08 ECAHA Montreal Wanderers 1908 – 09 ECHA Montreal Wanderers 1909 – 11 NHA	RS* PO*	60 14	x x	281 54	1 0	4.68 3.86
HOLMES, HARRY "HAP" Aurora, Ontario 1889 – 1940 Inducted 1972	Toronto Blueshirts 1912 – 1916 NHA Seattle Metros 1915 – 17 & 1918 – 1924 PCHA Toronto Arenas 1917 – 1919 NHL Victoria Aristocrats 1924 – 25 WCHL Victoria Aristocrats 1925 – 26 WHL Detroit Cougars 1926 – 28 NHL	RS† PO†	410 52	6510 420	1191 126	41 6	2.90 2.42
HUTTON, BOUSE Ottawa, Ontario? 1877 – 1962 Inducted 1962	Ottawa Senators 1898 – 1904 CAHL	RS* PO*	36 12	x x	106 28	2 2	2.94 2.33
LEHMAN, HUGH Pembroke, Ontario 1885 – 1961 Inducted 1958	Berlin Dutchmen 1908 – 1911 OPHL New Westminster Royals 1911 – 14 PCHA Vancouver Millionaires 1914 – 26 PCHA Chicago Blackhawks 1926 – 28 NHL	RS† PO†	403 48	3047 120	1451 137	23 7	3.60 2.85
LeSUEUR, PERCY Quebec City, Quebec 1882 – 1962 Inducted 1961	Smith Falls 1905 – 06 FAHL Ottawa Senators 1905 – 08 ECAHA Ottawa Senators 1908 – 09 ECHA Ottawa Senators 1909 – 14 NHA Toronto Shamrocks 1914 – 15 NHA Toronto Blueshirts 1915 – 16 NHA	RS† PO†	156 9	x x	718 40	4 0	4.60 4.44
LUMLEY, HARRY Owen Sound, Ontario 1926 – Inducted 1980	Indianapolis Capitols 1943 – 44 AHL Detroit Red Wings 1943 – 50 NHL Chicago Blackhawks 1950 – 52 NHL Toronto Maple Leafs 1952 – 56 NHL Boston Bruins 1957 – 60 NHL	RS PO	804 76	48097 4778	2210 199	71 7	2.76 2.50

	Games Played	Minutes	Goals Against	Shutouts	Average
MORAN, PADDY Quebec City, Quebec 1877 – 1966 Inducted 1958 Quebec Bulldogs 1901 – 05 CAHL Quebec Bulldogs 1905 – 08 ECAHA Quebec Bulldogs 1908 – 09 ECHA Haileybury Comets 1909 – 10 NHA Quebec Bulldogs 1910 – 17 NHA	RS† 201 PO† 7	x x	1094 24	2 1	5.44 3.43
PARENT, BERNIE Montreal, Quebec 1945 – Inducted 1984 Oklahoma City Blazers 1965 – 67 CPHL Boston Bruins 1965 – 67 NHL Philadelphia Flyers 1967 – 71 & 1973 – 79 NHL Toronto Maple Leafs 1970 – 72 NHL Philadelphia Blazers 1972 – 73 WHA	RS 608 PO 71	35136 4302	1493 174	55 6	2.55 2.43
PLANTE, JACQUES Shawinigan Falls, Quebec 1929 – 1986 Inducted 1978 Montreal Royals 1951 – 53 QSHL Buffalo Bisons 1952 – 54 AHL Montreal Canadiens 1952 – 63 NHL Montreal Royals 1960 – 61 EPHL NY Rangers 1963 – 65 NHL Baltimore Clippers 1964 – 65 AHL St. Louis Blues 1968 – 70 NHL Toronto Maple Leafs 1970 – 73 NHL Boston Bruins 1972 – 73 NHL Edmonton Oilers 1974 – 75 WHA	RS 837 PO 112	49533 6651	1965 241	82 15	2.38 2.17
RAYNER, CHUCK Sutherland, Saskatchewan 1920 – Inducted 1973 Springfield 1940 – 42 AHL NY Americans 1940 – 41 NHL Brooklyn Americans 1941 – 42 NHL NY Rangers 1945 – 53 NHL	RS 425 PO 18	25491 1134	1295 46	25 1	3.05 2.43
SAWCHUK, TERRY Winnipeg, Manitoba 1929 – 1970 Inducted 1971 Omaha Knights 1947 – 48 USHL Indianapolis Capitols 1948 – 50 AHL Detroit Red Wings 1949 – 55 & 1957 – 64 & 1968 – 69 NHL Boston Bruins 1955 – 57 NHL Toronto Maple Leafs 1964 – 67 NHL LA Kings 1967 – 68 NHL NY Rangers 1969 – 70 NHL	RS 971 PO 106	57114 6311	2401 267	103 12	2.52 2.54
THOMPSON, CECIL R. "TINY" Sandon, British Columbia 1905 – 1981 Inducted 1959 Boston Bruins 1928 – 39 NHL Detroit Red Wings 1939 – 40 NHL	RS 553 PO 44	34174 2970	1183 93	81 7	2.08 1.88
TRETIAK, VLADISLAV Moscow, USSR 1952 – Inducted 1989 Central Red Army 1969 – 84 Soviet National Team 1969 – 84	RS x PO x	x x	x x	x x	x x
VEZINA, GEORGES Chicoutimi, Quebec 1887 – 1926 Inducted 1945 Montreal Canadiens 1910 – 17 NHA Montreal Canadiens 1917 – 26 NHL	RS† 328 PO† 38	11564 1596	1145 122	15 4	3.49 3.21
WORSLEY, LORNE "GUMP" Montreal, Quebec 1929 – Inducted 1980 New Haven Ramblers 1949 – 50 AHL St. Paul Saints 1950 – 51 USHL Saskatoon Quakers 1951 – 53 WHL Vancouver Canucks 1953 – 54 WHL NY Rangers 1952 – 63 NHL Providence Reds 1957 – 58 AHL Springfield Indians 1959 – 60 AHL Quebec Aces 1963 – 65 AHL Montreal Canadiens 1963 – 70 NHL Minnesota North Stars 1969 – 74 NHL	RS 862 PO 70	50232 4080	2432 192	43 5	2.90 2.82
WORTERS, ROY Toronto, Ontario 1900 – 1957 Inducted 1969 Pittsburgh Pirates 1925 – 28 NHL NY Americans 1928 – 37 NHL Montreal Maroons 1929 – 30 NHL	RS 484 PO 11	30175 690	1143 24	66 3	2.27 2.09

Officials

ARMSTRONG, NEIL; Plympton Township, Ontario 1932 –; Inducted 1991
ASHLEY, JOHN; Galt, Ontario 1930 –; Inducted 1981
CHADWICK, BILL; New York City, New York 1915 –; Inducted 1964
ELLIOTT, CHAUCER; Kingston, Ontario 1879 – 1913; Inducted 1961
HAYES, GEORGE; Montreal, Quebec 1914 – 1987; Inducted 1988
HEWITSON, BOBBY; Toronto, Ontario 1892 – 1969; Inducted 1963
ION, MICKEY; Paris, Ontario 1886 – 1964; Inducted 1961

PAVELICH, MATT; Park Hill Gold Mines, Ontario 1934 –; Inducted 1987
RODDEN, MIKE; Mattawa, Ontario 1891 – 1978; Inducted 1962
SMEATON, COOPER; Carleton Place, Ontario 1890 – 1978; Inducted 1961
STOREY, RED; Barrie, Ontario 1918 –; Inducted 1967
UDVARI, FRANK; Yugoslavia 1924 –; Inducted 1973

Builders

ADAMS, CHARLES; Newport, Vermont 1876 – 1947; Inducted 1960
ADAMS, WESTON; Springfield, Massachusetts 1904 – 1973; Inducted 1972
AHEARN, FRANK; Ottawa, Ontario 1886 – 1962; Inducted 1962
AHEARNE, BUNNY; County Wexford, Ireland 1900 – 1985; Inducted 1977
ALLAN, SIR MONTAGU; Montreal, Quebec 1860 – 1951; Inducted 1945
ALLEN, KEITH; Saskatoon, Saskatchewan 1923 –; Inducted 1992
BALLARD, HAROLD; Toronto; Ontario 1903 – 1990; Inducted 1977
BAUER, FATHER DAVID; Kitchener – Waterloo, Ontario 1924 – 1988; Inducted 1989
BICKELL, J.P.; Toronto; Ontario 1884 – 1951; Inducted 1978
BOWMAN, SCOTTY; Montreal, Quebec 1933 –; Inducted 1991
BROWN, GEORGE Boston; Massachusetts 1880 – 1937; Inducted 1961
BROWN, WALTER Boston; Massachusetts 1905 – 1964; Inducted 1962
BUCKLAND, FRANK; Gravenhurst, Ontario? 1902 – 1991; Inducted 1975
BUTTERFIELD, JACK Regina; Saskatchewan 1919 –; Inducted 1980
CALDER, FRANK; Bristol, England 1877 – 1943; Inducted 1947
CAMPBELL, ANGUS; Stayner, Ontario 1884 – 1976; Inducted 1964
CAMPBELL, CLARENCE; Fleming, Saskatchewan 1905 – 1984; Inducted 1966
CATTARINICH, JOSEPH Levis; Quebec 1881 – 1938; Inducted 1977
DANDURAND, LEO; Bourbonnais, Illinois 1889 – 1964; Inducted 1963
DILIO, FRANK; Montreal, Quebec 1912 –; Inducted 1964
DUDLEY, GEORGE; Midland, Ontario 1894 – 1960; Inducted 1958
DUNN, JAMES; Winnipeg, Manitoba 1898 – 1979; Inducted 1968
EAGLESON, ALAN; St. Catherines, Ontario 1933 –; Inducted 1989
FRANCIS, EMILE "THE CAT"; North Battleford, Saskatchewan 1926 –; Inducted 1982
GIBSON, JACK; Berlin (Kitchener), Ontario 1880 – 1955; Inducted 1976
GORMAN, TOMMY; Ottawa, Ontario 1886 – 1961; Inducted 1963
HANLEY, BILL; Balleyeast, County of Antrim, Northern Ireland 1915 – 1990; Inducted 1986
HAY, CHARLES; Kingston, Ontario 1902 – 1973; Inducted 1974
HENDY, JIM; Barbados, British West Indies 1905 – 1961; Inducted 1968
HEWITT, FOSTER; Toronto, Ontario 1902 – 1985; Inducted 1965
HEWITT, WILLIAM; Cobourg, Ontario 1875 – 1966; Inducted 1947
HUME, FRED; New Westminster, British Columbia 1892 – 1967; Inducted 1962
IMLACH, GEORGE "PUNCH"; Toronto, Ontario 1918 – 1987; Inducted 1984
IVAN, TOMMY; Toronto, Ontario 1911 –; Inducted 1974
JENNINGS, WILLIAM; New York City, New York 1920 – 1981; Inducted 1975
JOHNSON, BOB; Minneapolis, Minnesota 1931 – 1991; Inducted 1992
JUCKES, GORDON; Watrous, Saskatchewan 1914 –; Inducted 1979
KILPATRICK, JOHN; —— 1889 – 1960; Inducted 1960
LEADER, AL; Barnsley, Manitoba 1903 – 1982; Inducted 1969
LEBEL, ROBERT; Quebec City, Quebec 1905 –; Inducted 1970
LOCKHART, THOMAS; New York City, New York 1892 – 1979; Inducted 1965
LOICQ, PAUL; Brussels, Belgium 1890 – 1947?; Inducted 1961
MARIUCCI, JOHN; Eveleth, Minnesota 1916 – 1987; Inducted 1985
MATHERS, FRANK; Winnipeg, Manitoba 1924 –; Inducted 1992
MCLAUGHLIN, FREDERIC; Chicago, Illinois 1877 – 1944; Inducted 1963
MILFORD, JAKE; Charlottetown, Prince Edward Island 1914 – 1984; Inducted 1984
MOLSON, SEN. HARTLAND; Montreal, Quebec 1907 –; Inducted 1973
NELSON, FRANCIS; —— Died 1932?; Inducted 1947
NORRIS, BRUCE; Chicago, Illinois 1924 – 1986; Inducted 1969
NORRIS, JAMES; Chicago, Illinois 1906 – 1966; Inducted 1962
NORRIS, JAMES SR.; St. Catherines, Ontario 1879 – 1952; Inducted 1958
NORTHEY, WILLIAM; Leeds, Quebec 1872 – 1963; Inducted 1947
O'BRIEN, JOHN AMBROSE; Renfrew, Ontario 1885 – 1968; Inducted 1962
PATRICK, FRANK; Ottawa, Ontario 1885 – 1960; Inducted 1958
PICKARD, ALLAN; Exeter, Ontario 1895 – 1975; Inducted 1958
PILOUS, RUDY; Winnipeg, Manitoba 1914 –; Inducted 1985
POILE, BUD; Fort William, Ontario 1924 –; Inducted 1990
POLLOCK, SAM; Montreal, Quebec 1925 –; Inducted 1978
RAYMOND, SEN. DONAT; —— 1880 – 1963; Inducted 1958
ROBERTSON, JOHN ROSS; —— 1841 – 1918; Inducted 1947
ROBINSON, CLAUDE; Harriston, Ontario 1881 – 1976; Inducted 1947
ROSS, PHILLIP; Montreal, Quebec 1858 – 1949; Inducted 1976
SELKE, FRANK; Kitchener, Ontario 1893 – 1985; Inducted 1960
SINDEN, HARRY; Collins Bay, Ontario 1932 –; Inducted 1983
SMITH, FRANK; Chatham, Ontario 1894 – 1964; Inducted 1962
SMYTHE, CONN; Toronto, Ontario 1895 – 1980; Inducted 1958
SNIDER, ED; Washington, District of Columbia 1933 –; Inducted 1988
STANLEY, LORD (OF PRESTON); London, England 1841 – 1908; Inducted 1945
SUTHERLAND, CAPT. JOHN T.; Kingston, Ontario 1870 – 1955; Inducted 1947
TARASOV, ANATOLI; Soviet Union 1918 –; Inducted 1974
TURNER, LLOYD; Elmvale, Ontario 1884 – 1976; Inducted 1958
TUTT, WILLIAM; Coronado, California 1912 – 1989; Inducted 1978
VOSS, CARL; Cheslea, Massachusetts 1907 –; Inducted 1974
WAGHORNE, FRED; Tunbridge Wells, England 1866 – 1956; Inducted 1961
WIRTZ, ARTHUR; Chicago, Illinois 1901 – 1983; Inducted 1971
WIRTZ, BILL; Detroit, Michigan 1929 –; Inducted 1976
ZIEGLER, JR., JOHN A.; Grosse Pointe, Michigan 1934 –; Inducted 1987

Select Bibliography

Coleman, Charles L. *The Trail of the Stanley Cup.* 3 vols. Montreal: National Hockey League, 1966–76.

Diamond, Dan, ed. *The Official National Hockey League 75th Anniversary Commemorative Book.* Toronto: McClelland & Stewart, 1991.

Diamond, Dan, and Joseph Romain. *Hockey Hall of Fame: The Official History of the Game and its Greatest Stars.* Toronto: Doubleday, 1988.

Dinger, Ralph, and James Duplacey, eds. *The National Hockey League Official Guide and Record Book 1992–93.* Montreal: National Hockey League, 1992.

Dryden, Ken. *The Game.* Toronto: Macmillan of Canada, 1983.

Fischler, Stan, and Shirley Fischler. *The Great Book of Hockey.* Lincolnwood. Ill.: Publications International, 1991.

Fitsell, J. W. *Hockey's Captains, Colonels, and Kings.* Erin, Ont.: Boston Mills Press, 1987.

Gallico, Paul. *The Golden People.* Garden City, N. Y.: Doubleday, 1965.

Germain, Georges-Hebert. *Guy Lafleur, l'Ombre et la Lumiere.* Montreal: Art Global/Libre Expression, 1990.

Hockey Hall of Fame Archives, Toronto, Ontario.

Hollander, Zander. *The Complete Encyclopedia of Hockey.* Detroit: Visible Ink Press, 1993.

Irvin, Dick. *The Habs.* Toronto: McClelland & Stewart, 1991.

McFarlane, Brian. *One Hundred Years of Hockey.* Toronto: Deneau, 1989.

Potvin, Denis with Stan Fischler. *Power On Ice.* New York: Harper & Row, 1977.

Young, Scott. *The Boys of Saturday Night: Inside Hockey Night in Canada.* Toronto: Macmillan of Canada, 1990.

Acknowledgements

Opus Productions Inc.:
President/Creative Director/Photographer: Derik Murray
Designer: Ken Koo, Ken Koo Creative Group
Design Studio Personnel: Jasana Crowie, Brian Daisley, Paul Despins, Maureen Schreiner, Shelley Stevens
Insert Photography: Perry Danforth and Grant Waddell, Derik Murray Photography Inc.
Photography Assistants: Nadia Molinari, Michael Morissette

Vice-President, Sales and Marketing: Glenn McPherson
Special Sales Representative: Gord Stellick

Vice-President/Project Director: Marthe Love
Author: Michael McKinley
Editor: Carolyn Bateman
Contributing Writer: Derik Murray
Production Coordinator: Wendy Darling
Editorial Assistant: Jennifer Love
Production Manager: Paula Guise
Administrative Assistant: Robin Evans
Project Accountant: Erma Main
Research: Andrew Bergant, Paula Guise, Alex Klenman, Douglas Love, Stefan Winfield
Statistics Research: The Learning Edge Corporation

Hockey Hall of Fame Research Consultant and Advisor: Philip Pritchard
Hockey Hall of Fame Research Consultants: Craig Campbell, Jeff Davis

Penguin Books Canada Ltd.:
President: Steve Parr
Vice President, Finance and Administration: Tim Man
Vice President, Sales and Marketing: Brad Martin
Publisher, Editor-in-Chief: Cynthia Good
Production Director: Dianne Craig
Editorial Associate: Mary Munro
Editorial Assistant: Cathy Leahy
Executive Assistant: Elizabeth McMullen

**A special thank you to KODAK CANADA INC. for their assistance on this project.
All photographs were shot exclusively on KODAK EKTACHROME Professional Films.**

Additional Photography Credits: Archival Black and White: Hockey Hall of Fame and McCord Museum of Canadian History, Notman Photographic Archives
Colour Player Photography: Bruce Bennett • Hockey Hall of Fame Exterior Photograph: Michael Morissette

Opus Productions would like to thank the following individuals and institutions for their invaluable assistance.
Alan Manzie • Angela Ryan • Audrey Grescoe • Bert Bell • Betty Murray • Book Art • Canadian Airlines • Cheryl Rielly, Canada Sports Hall of Fame •
Cliff Pickles, North South Travel • David Csumrik • David York • Dimitri Samaridis • Greg Harrison • Hal Eisen • Heather MacAuley, Royal York Hotel •
Heidi Von Palleske • Hugh Notman • Jack Grushcow • Jamie Engen • Janet Walkinshaw • Janice Lindsay • Jay Bajaj • Jay Currie • Jim Hughes •
John Taylor • Karen Love • Les Pioch • Lisa Morrison • Marge Lindsay • Matt Douglas • Mitchell and Sheldon Cohen, Mosaic Restaurant • Nancy Bell •
Nora Hague, Stanley Triggs, McCord Museum of Canadian History, Notman Photographic Archives • O'Brien family • Paramount Printing Group •
Pat Bidwell • Peter Scarth, Kodak Canada • Rainbow Graphic Arts • Rey Sandre • Robert J. Scott • Vistek Ltd. • Sandy Mitchell, Polaroid Canada •
Sharron Katz • Sue Love • Tom Best • Tom Gaston • Vern Harper, Cree Ceremonial Leader • Vintage Radio • Virginia Kelly • Waterford Communications

Hockey Hall of Fame Staff
Chairman: Scotty Morrison • President: A. David M. Taylor • Director, Finance and Operations: Jeffrey D. Denomme •
Director, Marketing and Communications: Phil Denyes • Facility Sales and Sponsorship Coordinator: Sue Bolender • Executive Assistant: Mary Carubia •
Retail and Merchandise Manager: Andy Yemen • Sales and Guest Services Coordinator: Bryan McDermott • Marketing Assistant: Christine Simpson •
Education and Group Program Coordinator: Ron Ellis • Manager, Resource Centre and Acquisitions: Philip Pritchard • Assistant Manager,
Resource Centre and Acquisitions: Craig Campbell • Archivist and Research Specialist: Jeff Davis • Resource Centre Services Assistant: Esther Richards •
Manager, Facility Systems and Exhibit Development: Ray Paquet • Facility and Exhibit Maintenance Coordinator: Barry Eversley •
Manager, Special Events: Scott North • Customer and Office Services Coordinator: Marilyn Robbins • Receptionist: Janice McCabe • Accounting
Supervisor: Sandra Buffone • Accountant: Sylvia Lau • Facility Services Assistant: Raymond Bruce • Photographer: Doug McLellan.

**The Hockey Hall of Fame, Opus Productions and Penguin Books Canada would also like to thank
the Honoured Members and all of the donors who have contributed to the Hall over the years.**

Index